Bible
Stories

10 BEST Bible Stories EVER!

Michael Coleman
Author of Foul Football

SCHOLASTIC

*FOR THE DAHLINKS – with thanks for
proving so brilliantly that the stories in Chapters 3
and 4 really can be performed on stage!*

Scholastic Children's Books,
Euston House, 24 Eversholt Street,
London, NW1 1DB, UK

A division of Scholastic Ltd
London ~ New York ~ Toronto ~ Sydney ~ Auckland

First published in the UK under the title *Top Ten*
by Scholastic Ltd, 1998
This edition published 2009

10 digit ISBN 1 407 10817 4
13 digit ISBN 978 1407 10817 9

Typeset by Rapid Reprographics Ltd
Printed and bound by CPI Bookmarque, Croydon, CR0 4TD

10 9 8 7 6 5 4 3

CONTENTS

INTRODUCTION

What's your favourite type of story?

How about blood-curdling adventures with buckets of blood? Or stories about heroic characters setting off on fantastic journeys and overcoming all sorts of dangers on the way? Maybe you prefer glittering historical stories featuring glamorous kings and queens – or grisly historical stories featuring gruesome kings and queens! Are amazing animal stories the sort you go for? How about a nice spooky ghost story, or one with a super-hero who's able to perform all kind of spell-binding tricks?

If you like any, or all, of these types of stories then the Bible is for you! It's packed with terrific tales featuring thousands of larger-than-life characters.

In this book you're going to be reading about the 10 Best stories and some of the characters who appear in the section of the Bible commonly known as the Old Testament by Christians, and the 'Scriptures' by Jews. These stories, together with dozens of others, fit together to make one big story, rather like the episodes of a serial on TV. This big story is the history of the Hebrews, a people we now know as the Jews.

Each of the 10 Best stories features a major character. There's one character, though, who is so important that he appears in all ten stories. His name is ... GOD.*

As far as the people who wrote the Bible were concerned, Hebrew history was God's history too. So, every story has got two sides to it – one, what actually happened to the characters in the story; and two, what God did and why. For instance, sometimes God was on the Hebrews' side, and sometimes he wasn't. On the occasions when he wasn't, the stories also try to explain the reason why God went off and left them.

The Bible is unique in being a sacred (holy) book to two major world religions: Judaism and Christianity. Both Jews and Christians believe that sections of the Bible are the 'word of God'. That is, they believe that, in some way, the many writers whose work makes up the Bible were all inspired by God to write what they did.

*How do you represent an invisible spirit (God)? The Old Testament writers used a number of ways: the top of a mountain, a cloud, a burning bush, a gentle breeze – even as a human being, walking in a garden. In this book we've decided to show him (as did Michaelangelo and plenty of other dead famous painters) as *An Old Man* in the *Sky*. This is why:

An = One, not many. For the Old Testament writers there's only one God.

Old = Timeless. God has to be older than everything – he created it all!

Man = 'He'. In the Bible, God is always referred to as a male.

Sky = Heaven. God lived in heaven. Nobody knew where heaven was, but high above the clouds seemed as good a place to think of as any.

Like many ancient stories, those in the Old Testament weren't written down to begin with. They were passed down from generation to generation by story-tellers. Ask your teacher about this. They do the same thing, telling new teachers about the terrible kids they've had in their class over the years. It was only in about 1000 BC that the first of these stories, poems and prayers started to be written down. After that, the collection grew continuously until the final books were written around 100 BC.

Since then the Bible has become far and away the best-selling book of all time. An estimated 6,000,000,000 copies have been produced. It's been translated into more than 2,000 languages, and the number is still growing.

You may or may not be pleased to know that the bits quoted from the Old Testament in this book are all taken from the modern translations The New International Bible or The Good News Bible and, for the Apocryphal* books, The Jerusalem Bible.

Time to get started, then! And you can't start at a time any earlier than that at which the Old Testament begins. Because it starts right at the beginning of time...

---

* Fourteen books included as an appendix to the Old Testament.

STORY 1: ADAM AND EVE (GENESIS 1:1 - 3:24)

The first book of the Bible is called Genesis. This is a Greek word meaning "first things" – which is fair enough since the opening chapters of Genesis tell the story of how God brought everything into being.

It's a story about four characters:

GOD – of course. The maker of absolutely everything

ADAM – the first man

EVE – the first woman

THE SERPENT – presumably the first serpent; definitely the first teller of whoppers

Nowadays this story is regarded by most people as being "mythical"; that is, it isn't meant to be a description of what actually happened, but a possible explanation of how everything in the universe came to be. "Everything in the universe" means what we can see, of course, from the stars in the sky down to the slimiest slug. But it also includes things that we can't see or accidentally tread on – things like good and evil.

So, not many people today believe that Adam and Eve were real people. But what if they were? What if an actual person called Adam did live, way back in the mists of time? And what if he'd kept a diary...

ADAM'S DIARY

Day 1 ......

Day 2 ......

Day 3 ......

Day 4 ......

Day 5 ......

Day 6.

Today I was created. I wonder why? According to God, my maker, I was the last job on his list. This is what he did before he got around to me: Phew!

GOD'S JOB LIST

Day 1.- Create the universe. Arrange day and night. [Or should that be night and day?]

Day 2.- Create heaven and earth. [Make sure earth sticks out of the sea.]

Day 3. – Create vegetation. [Decide about weeds!] 🌿

Day 4. – Create the sun and the moon ☀️ 🌙 [Sun to be the hot one. Moonbathing doesn't sound right.]

Day 5. – Create fish for the sea 🐠 and birds for the air. 🐦 [Do not confuse! Flying whales will be a major flop.]

Day 6. – Create all other animals. [Including man, if time.]

Day 7. – Very quiet. God is putting his feet up. He's whacked out, but pretty satisfied. He keeps saying that everything he's made is very good, especially me! Having had a first look at myself (there are puddles everywhere – God's been testing the rain all day) I have to say I agree with him.

Day 8. – Out of interest, I asked God how he made me. He said he gathered together a pile of dust, moulded me into shape, then breathed the breath of life into me. Blow me, what a beginning!

Day 9. – First thing this morning God took me to a place called the Garden of Eden. It's got all kinds of trees growing in it, all dripping with fruit and stuff. It's the most amazing garden I've ever seen. Not surprising, I suppose as it's the <u>only</u> garden I've ever seen!

Day 10. — I'm certainly getting on in the world. Yesterday it was a new home, and today God gave me my first job. Not bad for somebody who's only five days old!

I'm a gardener. I've got to look after the Garden of Eden. God said I've got to look after the trees and pull up the weeds. Or was it look after the weeds and pull up the trees? I'll ask tomorrow.

Day 11. — Look after the trees. And there's a bonus! "You can pick what you like from them," said God. "You're on," I said, making a bee-line for the best one of the lot.

"All except that one," said God before I get anywhere near it. "That's the Tree of knowledge of Good and Evil, otherwise known as the KOGE-tree. Eat a KOGE-fruit and you've 'ad it, Adam. You'll die. So hands off."

Day 12. — A nasty experience! Found myself talking to myself and wondered if I was going mad. Then I remembered — I've got to talk to myself, there's nobody else around! I mentioned it to God. He said he'd see what he could do.

Day 13. — What a day! God's idea of finding me a mate was to wheel in every creature he'd created and ask if I fancied any of them.

It soon got pretty confusing.

"How about this one?" he'd say.

"Not really," I'd say. "I preferred that one."

"What other one?"

"The one before the one before this one."

"Oh, this is hopeless," said God. "They'll have to be given names.

So I have to think up names for every living creature on earth! It was easy to start with. I made up little names like ant and bat and dog. But it got harder and harder. By the end of the day I was saying the first thing that came into my head. You should have seen the look on hippopotamus's face when he heard what he'd have to spell for the rest of his life.

And, after that, I still didn't fancy any of them as a mate. (Especially hippopotamus!)

"Why don't we sleep on it?" said God.

Day 14. – Woke up with a pain in my side and another creature _by_ my side!

"Wotcha," it said. "I'm Eve. I'm a woman. Wossisname, God, made me during the night. I'm your mate, mate."

"Wow!" I said.

Eve is really pretty. Prettier than the hippopotamus, that's for sure! In fact she looks a lot like me, except that she's got bobbly bits where I haven't and she hasn't got dangly bits where I have.

"Did he make you out of dust as well?" I asked.

"Nah. He made me out of one of your ribs."
That explains the pain in my side!

Day 15. — I've got a nasty feeling Eve could be a pain in the neck as well.

"So where's the action round here, Ad?" she says. "Where do all the cool cats hang out?"

"Same place as all the other animals," I say. Then I tell her the rules about us looking after the Garden and especially about not touching the KOGE-tree.

 "Oh, yeah? I dunno about that." She says. Then she cackles. "Dunno about the Tree of Knowledge! Get it?"

"No."
She went off for a look around. I'm still on my own!

Day 16. — I think Eve is making up stories. When she came back from one of her wanders this morning she said she'd been talking to a serpent!

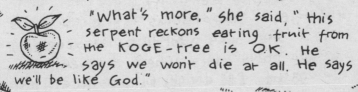

"What's more," she said, " this serpent reckons eating fruit from the KOGE-tree is O.K. He says we won't die at all. He says we'll be like God."

15

I ask you - a talking serpent!

Day 17. — Oh, dear! Eve's been and gone and done it! And so have I!

Eve had been gone such a long time that I went for a look around the garden. I found her under the KOGE-tree. That rotten serpent was with her.

"Go on," I heard it say, "have a bite." So Eve reached up, picked a fruit — and sank her teeth into it. Cor!

Then she handed it to me. "Go on, Adam. Have a bite."

"No, I mustn't. It's not allowed."

"Oh, what a wimp," said the serpent.

The next thing I knew — I'd done it! I waited to drop dead, but it didn't happen. I didn't even feel ill. But a funny thing did happen......... I suddenly felt embarassed. All I could think of was finding a fig leaf to cover up my dangly bits.

It wasn't just me, either. The fruit had affected Eve even more. She shot off and found three fig leaves!

I've got a nasty feeling that God is not going to be happy, though.

Day 18. — God was definitely

16

not happy.

"Adam!" he roared when he saw the fig leaves, "You've been eating KOGE-fruit, haven't you? That's why you've realised you're naked and covered yourself up!"

"It was Eve," I said. "She made me do it!"

"You rotten squinbag!" yelled Eve. "Anyway, the serpent made me do it!"

"I'm sorry, God," I pleaded. "We won't do it again. We'll both be good from now on. In fact — we'll both turn over a new leaf!"

God didn't laugh. I think we're in trouble.

Day 19. — We are in trouble. All three of us. God gave us the bad news one by one.

The serpent was first. He was condemned to crawl on his belly for ever. Talk about a long stretch!

Eve was next. God told her she's going to find it painful having children — or it might have been that her children are going to be a pain. Something like that.

Then it was my turn. "You're sacked, Adam," said God. He looked really sad about it! "You must leave the Garden of Eden. From now on you're going to have to work hard for your money. It doesn't grow on trees y'know."

So, that's the story. God made everything but he made things so that they'd be perfect. Human beings were his special triumph. The plan was that we would be like God and live happily together forever. Then, along came wickedness! But instead of saying "No thanks, I refuse to be tempted," humans said, "Oh, all right. I don't mind if I do!" This moment is known as "The Fall". It's saying that evil is in the world because of the way us humans behave. What's more, we know when we're being bad and this explains why humans aren't immortal, but die.

The story ends with a message of hope, though. Before they leave, God makes clothes for Adam and Eve – showing that, in spite of everything, God is still looking after his creation.

BIBLICAL BUT TRIVIAL: NO. 1

The lumpy bit that men have at the front of their throat is known as their Adam's Apple. It's based on the extra legend that the forbidden fruit stuck in Adam's throat.

Presumably women don't have one because Eve was a greedy hog and gulped her lump of fruit down whole!

FANTASTIC FACTS 1: WICKED WAYS

The story of Adam and Eve talks about Good and Evil. It tries to answer, in a very simple way, the question that is still posed today: if God exists, why is there evil in the world? Why are there murders and wars and plane crashes? Why are there earthquakes and floods?

So, here's your 10 Best run-down on Biblical goodies, baddies and absolute stinkers.

1. Goodie, goodie
Good, for the Old Testament writers meant every part of God's creation.

God saw all that he had made, and it was very good. (Genesis 1:31)

Everything in nature was good because all of it – trees, weeds, slugs, vultures, lions … even the serpent who tempted Adam and Eve – behaved the way God had intended.

2. Very very goodie goodie
Humans were also very good, – but only when *they* behaved the way God had intended them to. When they didn't, as Adam and Eve didn't, then they were acting in an evil way. And that was the big difference between

humans and the animal kingdom. For animals there was no such thing as right and wrong; they simply acted naturally. Humans, though, could choose to be good – or, like Adam and Eve, they could choose to be bad.

This ability to choose is called *free will*. Humans had been given it by God. It was up to them to choose to be good and it was part of what made them special.

3. Baddie, baddie

So what was evil? First and foremost the Old Testament writers taught that it was wrong for humans to get too high and mighty. God was the highest and the mightiest and to try to compete with him was not only wrong but would lead to big trouble.

The story of Adam and Eve is the first example of this. Another is the story of the Tower of Babel. It tells of a time when everybody spoke the same language.

Then they said, Come let us build ourselves a city, with a tower that reaches to the heavens, so that we may make a name for ourselves. (Genesis 11:4)

The story goes on to tell how God stopped them by giving them each a different language so that they couldn't understand each other. So when your teacher yells at you, "Stop babbling" (Babeling) you'll know what she means!

4. Yours sinfully

Doing wrong and being disobedient is called sin. You may have met the word before. Ice-hockey players who belt other players instead of the puck get sent to the "sin-bin" as a punishment.

Punishment and sin go together for the Old Testament writers, too. Any calamity had to be the result of somebody, somewhere, having been sinful.

5. Natural disasters

As the creator of all things it was believed that God could control everything in any way he wanted – especially to dish out punishment. So any calamity, like an earthquake or a flood, was seen as a punishment from God. Such disasters affected whole groups of people. A famous example is that which overtook the twin cities of Sodom and Gomorrah.

The Book of Genesis doesn't go into details about what went on there, other than to say that absolutely everybody was doing it. That's probably just as well, because it must have been awful if the punishment was anything to go by...

Then the Lord rained down burning sulphur on Sodom and Gomorrah... Early next morning Abraham... saw dense smoke rising from the land, like smoke from a furnace. (Genesis 19:24, 27)

The lesson was clear. If you're a sinful person, God will make it hot for you!

6. I don't feel well!

Of course it was also clear to everybody that sometimes people suffered even though they'd done nothing wrong. Illness was often seen in this way. If somebody fell ill, people asked: What have we done wrong?

If it wasn't obvious, then one answer was that somebody in their family must have done something wrong. It was believed that children could be punished for sins their parents committed! (Like you being kept in because your Mum didn't do her homework when she was at school!)

When it came to illness, the Old Testament wasn't talking about a bad cold, either. Have a look at this threatening list:

If you do not obey the Lord your God ... all these curses will come upon you and overtake you...

The Lord will strike you with wasting disease, with fever and inflammation, with scorching heat and drought, with blight and mildew, which will plague you until you perish. (Deuteronomy 28:21-22)

7. Why me?

There was another answer to the problem of why innocent people suffer, though. It is given in what is the longest story in the Old Testament: *The Book of Job.*

Job was a rich man. What's more, he was a good man. He hadn't done anything wrong. Not a thing. No reason for him to be picked on at all. And yet, as the story goes, God allows Job's faith to be tested by Satan.

– His cattle are stolen and some servants murdered.

– His sheep and more servants burned to a frazzle by a fire from the sky.

– His camels stolen and his last few servants murdered.

– His family killed when a wind blew their house down on top of them.

– Job himself is covered from head to toe in painful sores.

Does Job condemn God for all this? No. He says:

The Lord gave and the Lord has taken away; may the name of the Lord be praised! (Job 1:21)

He realises that he's being tested and that one day, just so long as he stays faithful to God, he'll get his reward. (This explains why sometimes your teacher may look round your class and moan: I must have the patience of Job to deal with you lot!)

And, at the end of the story, Job does get his reward. His riches are restored. God gives him a new family, double the possessions that were taken away from him, and he lives to be one hundred and forty!

This second answer, then, was that – hard as it might

be to appreciate – sometimes the innocent suffered because it was part of God's plan.

8. Good from evil

Linked to this was the idea that God could actually turn evil into good. The story of the Syrian army commander Naaman is an example.

Naaman had leprosy, a terrible skin disease. Hearing about the prophet Elisha, he travelled to Israel to meet him. Elisha sent him off to wash seven times in the river Jordan. Bingo – Naaman was cured. More than that, from the incident a greater good had come about; Naaman's conversion.

Then Naaman and all his attendants went back to the man of God. "Now I know that there is no God in all the world except in Israel." (2Kings 5:15)

9. The Devil

This idea, that God didn't send evil into the world as a punishment, developed very slowly in Hebrew thinking. When it did occur to them, though, it didn't actually solve the problem. It replaced it with another one. If God wasn't the cause of disasters and wickedness – who was?

There are many places in the Old Testament where it's suggested that when God wanted something done on earth he sent a messenger – "an angel" – to do the job. Forget the white robes and wings, though. The impression you get is that these were hit men. In fact, whenever disaster or disease were around, the chances were that an angel wasn't far away. The destruction of Sodom and Gomorrah, for instance, is presided over by two angels.

And who was it that brought Job all his problems? None other than The Devil – Satan – himself!

Although not fully developed in the Old Testament, this is the place where an evil opponent to God begins to take shape.

10. Heaven and Hell

What happened to the Hebrews when they died? Did they live on in some way? Was there some after-life?

For many years the Hebrews thought not. Their picture of the world was very simple.

Down below the earth was a place called "Sheol" (in English, this translates as "Hell") and this was where everybody – good or bad – went when they died.

So, the thinking went, if everybody ended up in the same rotten place God must dish out his rewards to those who've been good while they're alive. That's why riches and a long life were always thought of as blessings from God.

The trouble was, everybody knew somebody who'd been good but died young or poor, or both! There were also plenty of old, rich crooks walking about. Slowly the idea began to take shape that maybe only the baddies went to hell and the goodies – eventually, if not straight away – would end up somewhere a lot more comfortable.

Multitudes who sleep in the dust of the earth will awake: some to everlasting life, others to shame and everlasting contempt. (Daniel 12:2)

Good-y!... Except that it still left the same very tricky question that everybody who believes in heaven and hell still have to face: in which direction will God think I should go when I pop it? Up – or down!

BIBLICAL AND MIND-BOGGLING: NO. 1

The story of Adam and Eve ends with the snake being told that he'll have to crawl on his belly for the rest of his life. Just a fanciful tale to explain how snakes get around, you might think.

But did you know that, in prehistoric times, snakes almost certainly used to have legs? Zoologists have discovered that Pythons and Boa Constrictors still have hip bones!

What happened next?

After Adam and Eve are banished from the Garden of Eden, chapters 4 and 5 of the Book of Genesis go on to describe what happens.

They have two sons, named Cain and Abel ... until Cain murders Abel (the first murder).

Cain and Seth (another son) both marry and have children of their own.

This presents a small problem – where did their wives come from? The Old Testament doesn't say that Adam and Eve had any daughters! The answer is that the Old Testament stories weren't trying to tell a world history, but a history of the Hebrews. The fact that other people were around by this stage is taken for granted.

Cain and Seth certainly found a couple, anyway!

So the numbers of people on earth increase, showing that at least Adam and Eve did one of the things God told them to do: *"Be fruitful, and increase in number; fill the earth..."* (Genesis 1:28)

If you do some sums with the list of generations given

in Genesis 5:1-32, you'll discover that Adam and Eve's great-great-great-great-great-great-great-grandson was born 1,056 years after the Creation.

His name was Noah... But by that time God was getting pretty fed up with his creation...

STORY 2: NOAH
(GENESIS 6:5 - 8:22)

So the story goes, everywhere God looked he saw wickedness. Not just wicked actions, but wicked thoughts as well. What sort of wickedness? You want all the gory details? Bad luck. *The Book of Genesis* doesn't spell out what sort of wickedness, except for one particular thing – violence:

So God said to Noah, "I am going to put an end to all people, for the earth is filled with violence because of them." (Genesis 6:13)

Who was Noah? Together with his family, Noah was the one person in the world who God thought wasn't an absolute stinker.

So, God decides, start again. He decides to bring a great flood and destroy every living thing except for Noah, his wife, his three sons – Shem, Ham and Japheth – and their wives. Not unreasonably, he gives Noah a little bit of warning. Preparing for a calamity takes time, after all.

Here's how the story might have been told by one of Noah's sons…

OUR DAD BY SHEM, SON OF NOAH

Let's be honest, when it all started we wondered whether Dad was going a bit funny in the head. He was 600 years old, after all, and the brain-box does fade a bit as the years go by, doesn't it? Anyway, there we were at his birthday party, and what does he come out with? A chorus of 'Happy Birthday To Me'? Nothing like it.

"I'm going to make a boat," he says.

Mum says, "That's nice, dear. It'll keep you out of mischief."

"Yeah!" said my brothers, Ham and Japheth. "We can sail it on the pond!"

We all thought he was talking about a model boat, something he was going to knock up in the shed. It was only when he spread the plans across the table that we found out what he was really thinking of…

"Three hundred and fifty cubits long?" I said. "Fifty cubits wide? Thirty cubits high? What are you going to make, an Ark?" FOOTNOTE

"Yep," he says.

Then he told us what God had told him – that he thought his creation had turned all violent and horrible and that he'd decided to send a flood to get rid of everybody. Everybody, that is, except us! Well, as you can imagine, we were all a bit gob-smacked for a while. But when we thought about it we decided that if the rest of the world was like Eden then it *had* turned pretty gruesome.

You only had to go down to the shops to see that. People didn't seem to have time for each other any more. They'd just shout and swear until they got what they wanted. The roads weren't much better, either. Chariot-rage incidents were reported daily.

And come the night-time – well! It was a rare event for there *not* to be a punch-up outside the Eden Night Club. That's if you were mad enough to go out at night. Oh no, Eden definitely wasn't paradise!

So, Dad started work.

FOOTNOTE Maybe this footnote should be called an arm-note, because that's what a cubit was – a measure based on the length of an average arm. For a Hebrew arm that was apparently about 38 cms (15 inches). That means Noah's Ark was about 133 metres long (145yds), 22 metres wide (24yds) and 13 metres high (14yds).

Letter to the Editor of the Eden Gazette

Dear Sir,

I thought you might like to know that the end of the world is going to take place soon. There's going to be a great flood. This is bound to be a big event so you'll probably want to splash the news all over the front page.

Yours faithfully,

Noah.

Every day another cart-load of wood or reeds turned up at our house. You couldn't get in the front door for barrels of pitch. The neighbours used to stand in the street and laugh at Dad.

And, really, who could blame them? There wasn't a cloud in the sky and according to the weather forecast that's how it was going to stay.

But Dad carried on building. Slowly, his Ark began to take shape.

Until then I hadn't realised just how big 350 x 50 x 30 cubits was. When I saw the size of it, though, it suddenly occurred to me that it was a bit on the big side just for us. I soon found out why. It *wasn't* just for us!

"God's given me further instructions," said Dad after tea. "We've got to take two of every creature with us, one male and one female."

"Two of every creature?" says Ham.

"Yep," says Dad. "You've got to collect the animals. Jepheth's got to collect the reptiles, and Seth…"

"Don't tell me," I groaned, "I've got to get the fish, right?"

"The fish won't drown in a flood, dumbhead! You've got to catch the birds."

Well, we did it, but don't ask me how. I was just glad to have the birds. You should have seen the trouble Ham had getting a lead on his lion! And as for Japheth trying to sort out whether the lizard he'd caught was a boy or a girl...

Then, of course, there was the question of what they were going to eat. Since God's whole idea was that our cargo of creatures was going to be the mummies and daddies of all the new creatures on earth, we could hardly let them eat each other, could we?

Paradise Pet Stores,
Eden High Street,

Dear Sirs
            Please supply enough hay, seeds,
nuts, bananas etc. to feed two of
every creature in creation for about
9 months.
            Noah.

Needless to say, we were loading Dad's Ark for ages! Finally, though, we were all on board. Dad made some last minute arrangements.

Dear Milkman,
            Please cancel milk as from
next week.
            Noah.
P.S. Take my advice. Cancel your
own milk as well.

We were ready to set sail. The whole town turned up to wave goodbye. We stood on the top deck looking down at them. I could see their banners and flags and streamers and bunting. I could see them waving. There was only one thing I couldn't see.

Rain! There wasn't a cloud in the sky!

Our next-door neighbours, the Hardnuts, thought this was a hoot. But then they thought everything was a hoot, from pulling legs off spiders to smashing up the swings in Eden Park.

"Bon voyage," yelled Mr Hardnut. "Send us a postcard! A sea view!"

"I hope it stays dry for you!" laughed Mrs Hardnut.

A couple of the younger Hardnuts pointed up at the sun. "Hey, answer a riddle Noah," shouted one of them. "Why is the weather like a kettle?"

The other gave the answer, "Because it's boiling!"

And then, suddenly, it started raining.

There were just a few drops at first. Then more and more, as the rain got heavier and heavier. Soon the spectators were standing against the sides of the Ark to keep dry.

Once it started, it didn't stop. It rained for the rest of the day. And all night. And all the next day. And all the next day… Soon the water was lapping against the bottom of the boat. Still the rain didn't stop.

As the water rose higher and higher, Mr and Mrs Hardnut came running out of their house. "Can we come too?" they yelled.

"Jump in the lake!" yells Dad.

"That's not ferry nice! We're desperate! We're drowning!"

Dad wasn't too sympathetic. "It never rains but it pours," he laughed.

Slowly the water level rose. As the Hardnuts slowly sank out of sight, the Ark lifted off. We were on our way.

It was not a fun trip. After the excitement of surviving the flood, there was the business of surviving the boredom. I mean, it rained solid for forty days and nights. After all that time, "I spy something beginning with W" begins to lose some of its excitement!

Finally, though, the rain stopped. So Dad opened a porthole and sent out a raven to fly around. Then he sent out one of the two doves. They came back that evening.

"Didn't find anywhere to land," says Dad.

Seven days later he sends the dove out again. This time it comes back with an olive branch in its beak.

"Yeah!" shouts Dad. "Either the trees are getting taller or the water's going down."

"Just so long as we don't," says Mum.

Another seven days go by, and Dad sends out the dove again. This time it doesn't come back. Of course the other dove was well annoyed, but Dad says, "Ah, stop your squawking! You'll see your mate soon. It must mean there's some uncovered land out there somewhere. Journey's nearly over."

Nearly! It was 150 days before we finally landed. The

pong from below decks was evil. But, finally, the doors were opened and we all got off. Us, Noah's family, and two of everything God had created.

High up in the sky there was a rainbow. Dad pointed up at it. "Look at that," he yells. "It must be God's sign that we're saved. We've got to say thanks!"

So what does he do? Builds an altar and chooses some of the animals to sacrifice to God. I ask you! Saved from drowning, enduring one hundred and fifty days on board a floating crate, only to end up as a burnt offering!

The Covenant – Noah's Big Deal with God

Like the Creation story, the tale of a good man who survives a massive flood which drowns everybody else is one that's found in a lot of cultures.

So what's the big difference in the Bible's story about Noah? Once again, it's that the Old Testament writers have taken an existing and well-known story and turned it into a teaching about how humans and God work together. The wickedness of humans was the reason why God destroyed the world.

But God is merciful. If you're good (like Noah) then you'll be spared any of the nasty stuff.

In the Old Testament, this promise from God is known as a "covenant". The rainbow is the sign.

I have set my rainbow in the clouds, and it will be the sign of the covenant between me and the earth. Whenever I bring clouds over the earth and the rainbow appears in the clouds, I will remember my covenant between me and you and all living creatures of every kind. Never again will the waters become a flood to destroy all life. (Genesis 9:15)

As you'll see later, this is the first of many covenants God has to make with his people. (Why? Do you always keep your promise to tidy your room? There you go, then!)

BIBLICAL BUT TRIVIAL: NO. 2

According to the Old Testament, Noah's Ark was over 130 metres in length. That would have made it almost as long as a typical modern day navy destroyer – but the Ark would have been over 5 metres wider!

FANTASTIC FACTS 2: BIBLE ANIMALS

The story of Noah isn't the only place in which animals are mentioned in the Old Testament. They pop up everywhere.

1. Animal crackers
The animals most frequently mentioned in the Bible are:
- Farm animals like the sheep, lamb, goat and ram.
- Beasts of burden like the horse, ass, ox, bullock and camel.
- Wild animals like the wolf, bear and lion. But which of those animals gets the most mentions?

Answer:
The lion, with 167 mentions. This is because the image of the lion is often used in the Bible to describe something else, like:

A king's wrath is like the roar of a lion; he who angers him forfeits his life. (Proverbs 20:2)

Why? Because the people knew about lions. Go to Israel nowadays and you won't see one, but in Old Testament days lions roamed the Jordan valley looking for farm animals (and farmers) to eat. The Hebrews did the praying, and the lions did the preying!

COME ON LADS! LET US PREY!!

2. Loadsa Money

If you're a rich person nowadays, and you want everybody to know about it, what do you do? Head for the showrooms to buy a big car to park outside your front door, that's what. But what would have marked you out as a rich dude in Old Testament times? Lots of animals, or lots of servants?

Answer:

Lots of animals. Large herds were a symbol of power and wealth. Job is a good example. He had seven sons and three daughters, and he owned 7,000 sheep, 3,000 camels, 500 pairs of oxen and 500 donkeys, and he had a large number of servants. (Job 1:2)

Notice that the animals are mentioned before the servants? That's because animals were often worth more than slaves. Take a good horse, for instance, like King Solomon bought:

Solomon's horses were imported from Egypt ... for 150 shekels of silver (1Kings 10:28-29)

As a slave would cost you 30 shekels, that meant 1 horse was worth 5 slaves!

3. Who's vegetarian?

Test your teacher! Were the Hebrews vegetarians?

Answer:

Yes – and no! Based on the Old Testament, the Hebrews

were vegetarian until the time of the Flood, but meat-eaters afterwards! So, if your teacher answered "no", show him/her:

Then God said (to Adam): I give you every seed-bearing plant ... and every tree that has fruit with seed in it. They will be yours for food. (Genesis 1:29)

If he/she answered "yes", then show her what God said to Noah and his family after they left the Ark:

Everything that lives and moves will be food for you. Just as I gave you the green plants, I now give you everything. (Genesis 9:2)

4. Ugh! Dirty!

For the Hebrews, certain animals were called "unclean". This meant that they were not to be eaten. It was believed that those who did so would themselves become "unclean" – that is, not pure enough to follow God or be a member of the community. Anybody eating "unclean" food had to go through a ceremony to become "clean" again. (And you complain about having to wash your hands before eating your tea!)

So, which of these do you think were regarded as unclean?

1.	sheep	6.	spider
2.	grasshopper	7.	eel
3.	dog	8.	pig
4.	bat	9.	deer
5.	pigeon	10.	horse

Answers:
Clean: sheep, grasshopper, pigeon, deer;
Unclean: dog, bat, spider, eel, pig, horse.
Very roughly, a clean land animal was one which chewed the cud and had a cloven hoof – like sheep, goats, cattle or deer.

If it chewed the cud but didn't have a cloven hoof (like the hare) then, sorry, it was unclean.

Likewise, if it had a cloven hoof but didn't chew the cud (like the pig) then that was unclean too.

And if it didn't chew the cud or have a cloven hoof (like horses, dogs, snakes, rats and lions then it was definitely unclean).

Of the rest, most insects were unclean – with the exception of the grasshopper! – and so were fish that didn't have fins and scales. So jellied eels were out, too.

5. Burnt Offerings

No, not a school dinner, but another risk for Old Testament animals. For if you didn't end up on the table, you could end up as a sacrifice.

Sacrificing an animal meant killing it, cutting it up, and then burning it on an altar. Hebrews did this as a way of showing God they were grateful for something (like providing a good harvest). The poor animal wasn't too grateful, of course.

What sort of animals were candidates for the chop? Clean, unclean, or didn't it matter?

Answer:
Only extra-clean animals could be sacrificed. Not only did they have to follow the cloven-hoof-chewing-the cud rule, but they had to be the best of the flock.

If you were going to be an Old Testament animal then, the best thing by far was to be an unclean one. That way not only couldn't you be eaten, you couldn't be sacrificed either!

6. Harmful Animals
A number of animals were thought to be harmful. Insects such as gnats, flies and locusts were high on the list because they multiplied by the million and destroyed crops.

Snakes weren't appreciated either, not because they bit crops but because they bit people. After their escape from Egypt (see Moses in story 4) many of the Hebrews died from snake bites until God told them what to do. What was it?

Answer:
God told them:
Make a snake and put it up on a pole; anyone who is bitten can look at it and live. (Numbers 21:8)

DO NOT TRY THIS AT HOME WITH YOUR PET COBRA!

7. Animal Imagery – I: Aah!

Animals are often used by Old Testament writers to get their point across. For example, they often wanted to say to the people how wonderful life would be if only everybody would behave themselves, stop fighting and live together in peace. Here's how this is described in the *Book of Isaiah*. Which animals do you think will fit in the gaps?

The wolf will live with the =A=, the leopard will lie down with the =B=, the calf and the lion and the yearling together; and a little child will lead them. The =C= will feed with the bear... and the lion will eat straw like the =D=. (Isaiah 11:6-7)

Answers:
A = lamb, B = goat, C = cow, D = ox

Domesticated animals are the "goodies" of the Old Testament. The sheep, for instance, is used as an example of a creature that is gentle and does what its shepherd (God) tells it to do. (Read the 23rd Psalm.)

The opposite picture is given, too. After the nation of Israel was destroyed the prophet Jeremiah wrote:

Israel is a scattered flock that lions have chased away. (Jeremiah 50:17)

8. Animal Imagery – II: Grrr!

So is the lion an example of a "baddie"? Sometimes. In the Old Testament the lion stands for power and strength. Quite often they're used to describe the armies that are threatening Israel.

A nation has invaded my land… It has the teeth of a lion, the fangs of a lioness!

Other animals are used simply to represent bad things. When a man named Shimei started giving King David an earful, one of the King's supporters said:

Why should this dead *** curse my lord the king? Let me go over and cut off his head (2Samuel 16:9)

What animal was Shimei being compared to?

Answer:

A dog. Dogs aren't warm and floppy in the Old Testament. They're wild, noisy and some of their habits are so disgusting they get turned into memorable wise sayings:

As a dog returns to its vomit, so a fool repeats his folly. (Proverbs 26: 11)

Yuck!

9. Mythological creatures

Some animals referred to in the Old Testament don't actually exist. Leviathan, for instance, a sort of Biblical Loch Ness Monster, represents a dangerous enemy:

The Lord will punish with his sword ... Leviathan the gliding serpent, Leviathan the coiling serpent; he will slay the monster of the sea. (Isaiah 27:1)

And how about the cherubim? They're huge creatures, with:

Are they goodies or baddies?

Answer:
Goodies – even though they look bad.

The cherubim are mentioned almost 100 times in the whole Bible. They're God's guards. Their first mention is in the Book of Genesis, where it says they're given the job of stopping Adam and Eve getting back into the garden of Eden after God kicks them out.

Many holy places and articles are described as having cherubim statues near them or mounted on them. King Solomon's temple in Jerusalem, for instance, had two cherubim statues each with a wing span of 10 cubits (that's nearly 4 metres, or just over 12 feet)! And they were covered in gold – which must have meant they were as goodie as gold!

10. Animal Rights
Did animals have any rights?

Answer:
No. Animals served the ancient peoples and the Hebrews were no exceptions. They kept animals for what they could provide – milk and transport (when alive), meat and clothing (when dead). Add this to their use as sacrifices and you can see that most animals didn't live to a ripe old age.

BIBLICAL AND MIND-BOGGLING: NO. 2
Archaeologists have found a number of thick levels of mud at various places in the Bible lands. They provide clear evidence that catastrophic floods were quite common in the area.

What happened next?
In telling what happens after The Flood, the book of Genesis packs many more stories into a short space. It concentrates particularly on the descendants of Noah's son, Shem.

Ten generations after Noah a man called Abraham was born. Abraham is mega-special. He's known as the Father of the Hebrew nation. In about 1950BC he was living in the ancient city of Ur (on the river Euphrates in modern Iraq) when God gave him an order:

"Leave your country, your people and your father's household and go to the land I will show you. I will make you into a great nation and I will bless you; I will make your name

great…" (Genesis 12:1-2)

So Abraham went, together with his wife Sarah, nephew Lot, and all their servants and possessions, to look for this land God was talking about.

Abraham's wife, Sarah, had never been able to have children and now she's 90 years old. So both she and Abraham are pretty gobsmacked when God tells them they're going to have a son! He's to be called Isaac. Before Abraham dies, he arranges a marriage for Isaac with a girl named Rebecca. They have twin sons, Jacob and Esau. Esau is the elder by a few minutes, and that means that his is the "birthright"; that is, when Isaac dies Esau will get double shares of Isaac's dosh. More importantly as far as the Old Testament writers are concerned, Esau is the one with whom God's covenant will continue.

One day, Esau comes home after a day's hunting. He's starving, and Jacob has got some soup on the boil.

So Jacob suggests they do a deal – if Jacob gives Jacob his birthright, then Jacob will give him a bowl of soup. The soup must have been fantastic, because Esau agrees!

Jacob marries two wives, Rachel and Leah and collects two concubines as well. A concubine was a sort of "reserve" wife in case the proper ones didn't manage to have sons who could carry on the family name.

He needn't have worried. Apart from one daughter, Dinah, the rest of his children were all sons. Rachel gave him two. The concubines gave him two each. As for Leah, she put the others to shame by giving Jacob six sons, making twelve in all!

He loved them all, of course. But the one he loved best was Joseph...

STORY 3: JOSEPH (GENESIS 37:1 - 46:7)

Yes, out of his twelve sons, Joseph was Jacob's favourite. Jacob makes this pretty plain – and so does Joseph, all of which annoys his brothers so much that they decide to take matters into their own hands.

It's a story with every ingredient you could wish for in a thriller: attempted murder, treachery, blackmail, naughty goings-on, false imprisonment... In fact it's a story with so much going for it that it's a wonder William Shakespeare didn't get around to writing a play about it...

"MUCH ADO ABOUT JOSEPH OR WHAT A LOT OF BROTHER!

Cast:

Jacob: Dad

Joseph: Hero of the story

Reuben, Simeon, Levi, Judah, Issachar, Zebulun, Dan, Naphtali, Gad, Asher and Benjamin – Joseph's 11 brothers (Boo! Hiss!)

Potiphar: One of the Pharaoh's ophicials

Mrs Potiphar: Potiphar's wiphe

Pharaoh: Egypt's big phish

Baker: Responsible for Pharaoh's daily loaph

Butler: Responsible for serving Pharaoh's phood and drink

ACT 1 SCENE 1 – OUTSIDE JACOB'S HOUSE.
Crowds of girls surround Joseph and his brothers. Joseph is wearing his new coat.

Girl: Oh, Joseph! Thou lookest the coolest!

Joseph: Too right, baby.

Brothers: (TOGETHER) Grrr!

Joseph: Dad gave it to me. I'm his favourite son, see-est?

Brothers: (TOGETHER) Grrr!

Joseph: There's no point you lot going Grrr! Thou knowest it's true. I am destined for great things.

Reuben: Thou art destined for a thick ear if thou dost not wrap up!

Joseph: I am wrapping up – in my nice new coat!

Brothers: (TOGETHER) Grrr!

ACT 1 SCENE 2 – NEXT MORNING.
All the brothers are in one very big bed.

Joseph: Here, dost thou lot want to hear about the dream I had last night?

Brothers: (TOGETHER) No

Joseph: Well, I dreamt we were all gathering and binding corn. Each of us had a sheaf. And guess what? All thy sheaves bowed to my sheaf! Wheat dost thou think it means?

Brothers: (TOGETHER) Snore, snore.

Joseph: I think it can only mean I'm going to be a big sheaf one day – ha-ha! Get it? Big sheaf, big chief!

Brothers: (TOGETHER) Snore, snore.

Joseph: Which means, compared to me, thou lot are going to be complete peasants.

Brothers: (WAKING UP TOGETHER) Grrr!!

ACT 1 SCENE 3 – OUT IN THE COUNTRY.
The brothers enter stage left with their herds of sheep and goats. Joseph enters, stage right, his coat over his shoulder.

Simeon: Oh, fiddlesticks. It's Joseph. I hatest him!

Levi: Me too-est.

Reuben, Judah, Issachar, Zebulun, Dan, Naphtali, Gad, Asher, Benjamin:
Me too, me too, me too, me too, me too, me too, me too, me too.

Issachar:	Let's run away from him, fast.
Zebulun:	No, let's call him rude names.
Judah:	No, let's kill him.
All:	Good idea!

Joseph approaches. Dramatic music from the orchestra as Joseph is jumped on. A knife is poised to strike.

Reuben:	Hang on! I'm the eldest and I'll get told off something wicked if he gets killed. I know, let's teach the little drip a lesson and chuck him down that well over there.

They do it. Reuben exits stage left with a herd of sheep. A group of traders enter down stage, riding camels. The other brothers start talking.

Dan:	Here, I've got a brilliant idea. Let's sell him to these traders!
Naphtali:	Like it! That way we get rid of Joseph...
Gad:	...and get enough cash to buy ourselves new coats!

Joseph is pulled from the well and given to the traders. Money changes hands. Tied to a camel, Joseph is led away.

Joseph: I've really got the hump with you lot!

Reuben enters stage left. He looks in the well.

Reuben: Well, well! He's escaped!
Asher: No, he hasn't, we've sold him.
Reuben: Sold him! Thou rotten lot! That's terrible! Awful! Oh, how dost the arrow of grief pierce my heart and fillest my eyes with saddest tears! Oh, thou pain! Oh, thou agony! Oh...
Asher: And here's your share of the dosh.
Reuben: Oh... thanks very much. Right, what am I going to tell Dad? Thinkest thou hard, brothers, thinkest thou hard.

A goat enters stage left.

57

| **Goat:** | Here, who are you looking at? |
| **Reuben:** | You! |

The brothers surround it. A knife is poised.

| **Goat:** | Oh, sometimes you lot really get my goat. Agggh! |

The goat is dismembered. (Props dept: be sure to order plenty of goats if the play is scheduled for a long run, because the goat won't be.)

ACT 1 SCENE 4: AT THE DINNER TABLE. *The brothers enter, one by one.*

Jacob:	Eight, nine, ten, eleven... eleven. Who's missing?
Reuben:	Er, Joseph, Pops. He kind of had an accident.
Simeon:	A lot of accidents actually. With a lot of wolves.
Levi:	We're all really chewed up about it, Dad.
Judah:	Not as much as Joseph is though!

Jacob: What ... thou meanest...

The brothers bring out Joseph's coat. It's ripped up and there's blood all over it.

Reuben: Yep. We are the meanest. Er... I meanest yes, we do meanest what thou think we meanest.

Naphtali: Our dear brother Joseph is no more.

ALL: Boo-ha-ha-hoo!

END OF ACT 1

ACT 2 SCENE 1: AN EGYPTIAN MARKET.
A number of slaves are being sold, Joseph among them. Potiphar and Mrs Potiphar, are looking on.

Trader: OK, let's not messest about here. What am I offered for this Mark I Joseph? Lookest thou at him. Lovely model, regularly serviced, good little runner. Comes complete with six months slave tax. An absolute bargain.

Potiphar: What thinkest thou, my love?

Mrs Pot: Mmm. Nicest bodywork, dearest. I'll take him!

ACT 2 SCENE 2: POTIPHAR'S BEDROOM. *Joseph is sweeping the floor. Mrs Pot arrives, looking slinky.*

Mrs Pot: Why, hello Jo!

Joseph: Hello Mrs P. I've done thy washing and thy ironing, so I thought I'd run around in here.

Mrs Pot: Just what I was thinking.

Joseph: I like it here Mrs P. Especially now Mr P. has put me in charge.

Mrs Pot: Oh yes, Jo, thou art top of the Pots where he's concerned. Now – give us a kiss!

Joseph: A kiss? Mr P. hasn't got that on my job list.

Mrs Pot: No, but I've got it on mine! Now, come here!

She grabs Joseph and is giving him a sloppy snog when Potiphar enters.

Potiphar: What's going on here-est, dearest?

Mrs Pot:	Woe, woe, it's due to Jo! He started it, darling. He wanted to kiss me. I said, "No, Jo," but he wouldn't listen. He got too hot, Pot!
Potiphar:	Right-oh! To jail you go, Jo!

ACT 2 SCENE 3: PRISON CELL.
Joseph between two other prisoners, the Pharaoh's butler and his baker. They're eating their breakfast...

Joseph:	Stale bread and water. I hate it!
Butler:	Me, too. As Pharaoh's butler, I'm used to far better phare.
Baker:	And I'm used to the nicest, phreshest bread.
Joseph:	So why did Pharaoh phrow – I mean, throw thee in here, Mr Baker?
Baker:	He was in a crusty mood. He'll let me out soon – I hope.
Butler:	Dream on!
Baker:	Funny thou should sayest that. I did have a dream last night.
Joseph:	Tellest me more. I'm good at

	dreams. I'll tellest thou what it meant.
Baker:	Well, I dreamt I was carrying three trays of cakes on my head...
Butler:	Obvious – thou hast something on thy mind!
Baker:	No, there's more. Birds came down and scoffest them all. I wonder what it means.
Joseph:	Bad news, bakey-baby. It means in three days time thou art going to be executed. Thou shalt lose thy loaf.
Butler:	What about me? I had a dream too. I dreamt that I squeezed the grapes from three branches into Pharaoh's cup and he drank it.
Joseph:	No probs. In three days thou shalt be out of here and butlering again.
Butler:	Yeah? Wow! I'll drinkest to that!
Joseph:	Hey – and when thou dost get out, don't forget who toldest thee the meaning of thy dream.

ACT 2 SCENE 4: PHARAOH'S PALACE.
It is some time later, after the Pharaoh's butler has been released from prison as Joseph predicted. Pharaoh is not happy. He's

had a bad night. He's in his pyjamas and groaning. The butler enters.

Pharaoh: What a night! I dreamt I saw seven fattest cows followed by seven thinnest ones. They were coming out of the river.

Butler: Come on! Pull the udder one, Sire!

Pharaoh: It's true, I tell you! Butler, fetch me somebody who can tell me what that cow-dream means. Go on, moo-ve!

Butler: Sire, I knowest just the man!

(EXITS HURRIEDLY)

ACT 2 SCENE 5: *The Butler enters with Joseph.*

Pharaoh: Right, Joseph. Seven fattest cows followed by seven skinniest ones. What does it mean?

Joseph: Pharaoh, the seven fat cows mean Egypt is going to have seven years of good harvests. Plenty of grub, Sire. After that there's going to be seven years of famine, though. That's what the seven thin cows stand for.

Pharaoh: Well, there's no point beefing about it. What dost thou suggest?

Joseph: Obvious. Find thyself a good organiser, somebody who can save enough in the first seven years to gettest the country through the next seven.

Pharaoh: Thou've gottest the job, Jo!

END OF ACT 2

ACT 3 SCENE 1: THE PHARAOH'S PALACE, *14 years later. The table is piled high with good food.*

Pharaoh: Well done, Joseph! We'd never have got through this famine without thee. I bet they're all starving to death outside Egypt!

Joseph: Yes, Sire...
(THOUGHTFUL LOOK)

ACT 3 SCENE 2: JACOB'S HOUSE.
Jacob and the eleven brothers are sitting at the table. They each have a plate in front of them. Jacob's plate has got one bean on it. The others have none.

Jacob: Let's face it, boys. We're in trouble.

Brothers: (TOGETHER) You're telling us! We haven't got a bean!

Jacob: Then there's only one thing for it. Thou will have to go to Egypt and buy some food for us. Go on, chop-chop!

ACT 3 SCENE 3: JOSEPH'S OFFICE.
The eleven brothers enter.

JOSEPH: (SHOCKED) It's my brothers!

Reuben: (BOWING LOW) We knowest we dost not lookest the prettiest, Your Greatness. That's because we art starving. We've come to buy food for ourselves and our father. He's hungry too, the poor thin.

Joseph: (ASIDE) They don't recognise me! Right, let's see if they've changed.

Benjamin: Sell us some corn, Your Goodness, before we flake out.

Joseph: OK-est. Hand over thy money and thy sacks. (ASIDE) Now for some fun!

Grain is put into the sacks. Eerie music as Joseph sneaks a gold cup into the sack of Benjamin, the youngest brother. The sacks are returned to the brothers.

Reuben: Thankest thou, your Goodness Graciousness. Thou art an absolute star. See-est thou later.

The brothers go to leave. Suddenly Joseph's voice rings out.

Joseph: Wait! My gold cup is missing!

Reuben: Well none of us have got it! We haven't seen thy cup. Or thy saucer.

Joseph:	A likely story. If thou lot haven't got it, who hast?
Judah:	Searchest me.
Joseph:	Right, I will. And the rest of thee.

The brothers' sacks are searched in turn until, finally, Benjamin's sack is reached. Dramatic roll of drums as Joseph pulls out the cup.

Benjamin:	I don't know how it got there! It wasn't me! I'm too young to drink!
Joseph:	Gotcha! Thou art staying here, mate. The rest of thee can go back to thy father and tell him he's lost a son.
Judah:	Sire, we can't go back without Benjamin. Thou see-est, we've mislaid a brother before. If we do it again, our father will drop deadest. Keep me instead, but let Benjamin go back.
Joseph:	(ASIDE) That's good enough for me. They're not the rotten bunch they were. (TO JUDAH) Dost thou not recognise me?
Judah:	No.
Joseph:	Lookest thou carefully, noodle!
Judah:	It... thou... art... thou... it's...
Joseph:	Joseph. Told you I was going to be a big sheaf, didn't I?

At this, the brothers clutch each other. Jacob enters stage left and clutches Joseph too. Handkerchiefs, noses blown ad lib.

THE END.

What Art It All About?

The story of Joseph has more than one meaning. As a straightforward story, its message is that if you stay faithful to God, then all will be well in the end. God will eventually help you out – although it may take some time!

It's also a tale which shows God keeping together a family who are always arguing and fighting. This was important for the writers of the Old Testament because the Hebrews were just like a big family. They weren't drawn from one group of people but from many tribes, and for that reason they didn't always agree with each other (if you've got brothers or sisters you'll know the feeling!). So, for the Hebrews, the religious message of the story was: if we stay faithful to God, he'll keep us together come what may.

The other feature of the story is historical. After Jacob and the brothers are reunited with Joseph they all move to Egypt. In this way the story reflects Hebrew history as it had been passed down from generation to generation – that, after famine hit Canaan, the people went to live in Egypt.

BIBLICAL BUT TRIVIAL: NO. 3

On 1st march 1968 in a London junior school, a musical version of Joseph's story was premiered. Since then the musical has been playing at theatres throughout the world: 'Joseph and The Amazing Technicolour Dreamcoat'!

IT'LL NEVER CATCH ON!

FANTASTIC FACTS 3: HAPPY FAMILIES

Joseph's story is about a family argument which went a bit further than name-calling or giving your brother or sister a quick poke in the ribs while Mum and Dad aren't looking.

So, what was it like to be a member of a large family in Biblical times? Was it easy or tough? Who was the boss? And what was a family anyway? Here are the family facts!

1 Big family

In Jacob's time, a family wouldn't just have been thought of as husband, wife (or wives!) and children. It would have included grandparents, uncles, aunts, cousins – and any servants the family might have. This made for BIG families! The *Book of Genesis* tells the story of Abraham, Jacob's grandfather, setting off to rescue his nephew Lot after he'd been kidnapped...

When Abraham heard that his relative had been taken captive, he called out the 318 men born in his household and went in pursuit... (Genesis 14:14)

Add on the untrained men, the women and children and you can see how big a family could be. How did he remember all their birthdays?

2 Do what I say, or else – I

WARNING: THIS SECTION NOT TO BE READ BY NERVOUS BOYS!

The boss of a family was the father. And boss is the right word. A father's word was law. He had total control over his children. If they were disobedient, it could mean a lot more than a clip round the ear...

If a man has a stubborn and rebellious son who does not obey his father and mother ... they shall say to the elders "This son of ours is stubborn and rebellious. He will not obey us..." Then all the men of his town shall stone him to death. (Deuteronomy 21:18-21)

3 Do what I say, or else – II

WARNING – THIS SECTION NOT TO BE READ BY NERVOUS GIRLS!

A father who was a bit hard up had a very easy way of making some money. He could sell his daughter as a slave! One girl who wasn't even that lucky was the daughter of a warrior named Jephthah. His story is told in the book of Judges 11-12. Before a battle he makes God a promise: that if he's victorious he will offer as a sacrifice whatever comes out of his house to meet him when he returns home.

Jephthah wins, returns home – and who should rush out to give him a big kiss but his only daughter!

4 Are you listening?

Nowadays parents tell their children things like: "Money doesn't grow on trees". If you want to know what Old Testament parents were saying to *their* children, then the *Book of Proverbs* is the place to look. Here's the 10 Best!

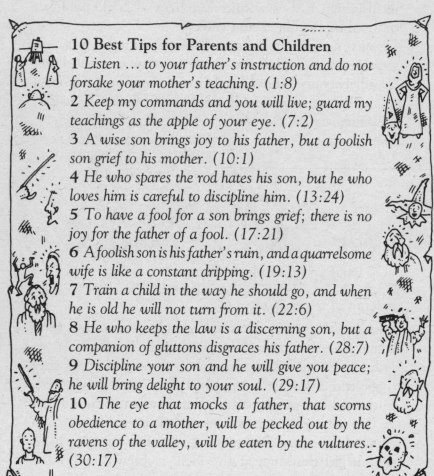

10 Best Tips for Parents and Children

1 *Listen … to your father's instruction and do not forsake your mother's teaching.* (1:8)

2 *Keep my commands and you will live; guard my teachings as the apple of your eye.* (7:2)

3 *A wise son brings joy to his father, but a foolish son grief to his mother.* (10:1)

4 *He who spares the rod hates his son, but he who loves him is careful to discipline him.* (13:24)

5 *To have a fool for a son brings grief; there is no joy for the father of a fool.* (17:21)

6 *A foolish son is his father's ruin, and a quarrelsome wife is like a constant dripping.* (19:13)

7 *Train a child in the way he should go, and when he is old he will not turn from it.* (22:6)

8 *He who keeps the law is a discerning son, but a companion of gluttons disgraces his father.* (28:7)

9 *Discipline your son and he will give you peace; he will bring delight to your soul.* (29:17)

10 *The eye that mocks a father, that scorns obedience to a mother, will be pecked out by the ravens of the valley, will be eaten by the vultures.* (30:17)

5 I do...

A father's authority over his sons and daughters lasted until they got married. So how old did a boy have to be before he could get married and start bossing his own wife and children about? Thirteen is the answer. Girls didn't even have to wait that long – they could get married when they were twelve!

Why so young? Because at twelve, most girls are capable of having a baby. Boys, the slow-coaches, can't usually become fathers until they're about thirteen. And remember what God said to Adam and Eve: "*Be fruitful, and increase in number; fill the earth ... Have many children, so that your descendants will live all over the earth.*" (Genesis 1:28) Allowing children to marry as soon as they could have children meant that no time was lost!

6 Because I say you do!

You didn't have a say in when you got married – or, even worse, who you got married to! That was decided by your father. So if you were unlucky, you could get stuck with a diabolical dimbo with a pot-belly and black moustache. Girls could get stuck with somebody even worse!

The idea behind it was that Dad knew best. Left to themselves, youngsters might go off and marry any old boy or girl they met at the local Hebrew Hop. But if Dad sorted out arrangements then a suitable husband or wife would always be found. What was 'suitable'? Lots of things came into it, like lots of money, but by far the most important was finding a husband or wife with the same belief in God.

7 What's she worth, then?

Once a marriage had been agreed, the two fathers would sit down and agree a *mohar* or marriage price. This was paid by the boy's father to the girl's father. This was to make up for the fact that, in letting her go, the girl's father had lost a good worker! The price didn't have to be money; Jacob worked for his wife's father Laban instead.

A gift went in the other direction, too. The bride's father would agree to give his daughter and her husband-to-be a "dowry" or wedding gift when they married. Just like wedding gifts nowadays, this would be something really useful. Forget automatic tea-makers and fifty-piece dinner services, though. "Useful" in Old Testament times meant something like a plot of land, or a servant, or maybe just a couple of sheep!

8 Two sheep, one wife... or more...

A man didn't just marry his wife, he *owned* her. She became one of his possessions, along with his animals.

For a long period of time a man could have as many wives as he wanted – or, more likely, could afford (they cost money, remember). For this reason it tended to be the kings and rich people who had more than one wife. What's more, if a wife was unable to have children – or if this appeared to be the case because she hadn't had any yet – then a man could take a concubine. Jacob, as we've seen, had two wives and two concubines. King Solomon, many years after Jacob, took the practice to its limits: *He had seven hundred wives of royal birth and three hundred concubines. (1Kings 11:3)*

What was the situation for a woman? Her choice was a lot simpler: one husband – or none! And, as it happens, that's how the practice came to be for a man, too. God's will came to be seen as the picture given in the story of Adam and Eve – one man with one wife...

9 I divorce thee!

A man was allowed to divorce his wife if he became unhappy with her for any reason However, divorce certainly wasn't encouraged. It probably didn't happen all that often either, if only because it was expensive. A man who divorced his wife had to pay back the dowry that they had been given and usually give her extra money as well.

Needless to say, a wife couldn't divorce her husband. She just had to put up with him.

10 Have you made a will, Daddy?

What happened to everything a father owned when he died? The answer is that his property was shared out amongst his sons. Sorry, girls, nothing for you yet ... but read on.

The eldest son received a double share. This was called the eldest son's birthright.

Here it is, girls. Your owner, your Dad, has just popped off. So what happens to you? Freedom? Afraid not. You get a new owner – your brother! And if you were the wife of the man who'd died? Then your new owner was your son!

A girl's only way of inheriting was to hope that her parents didn't produce any brothers for her. Maybe that's why sisters think they're brothers are so awful nowadays!

BIBLICAL AND MIND-BOGGLING: NO. 3

In Biblical times it was very unusual indeed for a man to be unmarried. In the Hebrew language, there is no word for 'bachelor' – an unmarried man.

What happened next?

Jacob's family pack their bags and move to Egypt. Genesis says that 66 of Jacob's extended family made their home there. Joseph married and had two sons – Ephraim and Manasseh, bringing the total to a nice round 70.

Thanks to Joseph, who uses his influence and power, they all settle down happily. Thereafter, descendants are called 'Israelites'.

For the next 400 years Joseph and Joseph's brothers marry, have children, their children have children etc, etc, and the Israelites grow to such numbers that they begin to think of themselves as "the Nation of Israel". And that's when the BIG trouble begins...

HI FAMILY! WELCOME TO EGYPT! COO! THERE'S A LOT OF YOU, AREN'T THERE?!!

STORY 4: MOSES (EXODUS 2 - 16)

It's a very sad story. A group of people come along and settle in a place. They make a real success of things – but the more successful they are, the more the people who were there first dislike them. (Read the newspapers – it's still going on today).

According to the *Book of Exodus*, this is what happened to the Israelites in Egypt. Eventually a Pharaoh came along who saw them as a threat and decided to give them a hard time. He started to persecute them, turning them into slaves and the like. Things got so bad that the Israelites decided they had to get away. All they needed to do was to find a strong leader who could help them. And they found one. Of all the figures in the Old Testament, Moses is the Big Star. So big, that if he'd been around today he'd definitely have a TV presenter with a big red book come up to him and say...

"MOSES, THIS IS YOUR LIFE!"

Compere: Moses, this is your life. You were born in Egypt, correct?

Moses: Yeh.

Compere: Not a very good time to be born, in fact?

Moses: Nah.

Compere: Pharaoh had just decreed that all boys under the age of one year should be killed. But you escaped.

Moses: Yeh.

Compere: Well, obviously you did, otherwise we wouldn't be doing this show would we? Ha-ha. Yes, you escaped and it was all thanks to the efforts of two women...

Disembodied voice from behind somewhere

1st voice: Me.

2nd voice: And me.

Compere: Do you recognise those voices, Moses?

MOSES: Nah.

Compere: Well, I'm not surprised. You haven't seen either of them for almost 120 years. Come in – your two mothers!

Two women enter.

Compere: Tell us what happened all those years ago.

1st mum: Moses was my baby. But I knew he was in danger, what with that rotten, mouldy Pharaoh…

2nd mum: Oi, that's my Dad you're talking about!

1st mum: Anyway, to keep him out of Pharaoh's clutches, I put Moses in a basket and floated him off down the River Nile.

Compere: Sink or swim, eh? Ha-ha. And you found him, Pharaoh's daughter?

2nd mum: Yes, I did. I thought, ooh, here's a little basket, I'll bring him up as my very own.

Compere: But you enlisted some help?

2nd mum: Well, yes. I didn't fancy all those nappies and smelly things. So I got a lady who'd just lost her son to help out.

1st mum: That was me! And I couldn't say anything about being his real mother or I would have given the game away! But now I can. Moses is mine. I want him back!

2nd mum: Well, you can't have him! So there!

They exit, fighting.

Compere: Anyway, Moses. You grew up to be big and strong. A handsome chap with rippling muscles. A strong, silent type.

Voice: It's him! He fits the description!

Compere: He's been hunting you for over 100 years. Come in, Inspector Ahab of the Egyptian Police!

Inspector Ahab storms on, looking determined.

Ahab: It's him. It's definitely him. He killed an Egyptian who was mistreating an Israelite, then hopped it. Admit it, you're him aren't you?

Moses: Yeh.

Ahab: Well, you can't be done for it now. Not 100 years later. But just put me out of my misery. Where did you go to?

Voices off: He was hiding with us!

Compere: Yes, it's the new family you found in Canaan. Come in, wife Zipporah, sons Gersham and Eliezer, and father-in-law Jethro!

The family enter.

Jethro: Moses looked after my flocks. And was pretty good at it.

Zipporah: Until the day he went up that mountain at Horeb.

Gersham: Then he came rushing home. "Where's the fire?" I said. And he says, "Up there!"

Eliezer: Then he tells us. He's heard the voice of God coming out of a burning bush!

Jethro: Saying, "Go back to Egypt, Moses. Tell the Pharaoh to let my people go!"

Zipporah: (GRABS MOSES BY THE THROAT) A likely story, husband! You wait till this show's over. I want the truth out of you. Leaving me to bring up our children and a flock of sheep on my own...

Compere: Thank you, Zipporah and everybody! Looks like you've got some explaining to do, Moses. Ha-ha! So, back to Egypt you went. But you weren't alone...

Zipporah: I knew it! Another woman...

Compere: Thank you, Zipporah!

They all go out, Zipporah glaring at Moses and muttering about divorce.

Compere: Now, Moses. When you were at the top of the mountain you told God you were a man of few words, right?

Moses: Er ... yeh.

Compere: And so he sent somebody with you to Egypt to do the talking.

Voice off: That's right, it was me, y'know, like. Me, myself.

Compere: Come in, your brother Aaron!

Aaron enters.

Aaron: Well, see, I could always talk better than ol' Moses here, so God says, goo-on my son, he says, get in there! So I did, like, know what I mean?

Compere: And so, Moses, you went to the Pharaoh and asked him to let the Israelites go.

Moses: Yeh.

Compere: And what did he say?

Moses: Nah.

Aaron: So then I says to Pharaoh, I says: listen Pharaoh, these lads want out, away, right? Be sensible, I said, just let 'em go and there'll be no trouble, y'know what I mean? And y'know what he said?

Voice off: Make me.

Aaron: That's right!

Compere: That's the voice of Pharaoh. Unfortunately, he can't be with us tonight. Well, to be honest, he didn't *want* to be with us tonight. He said he never wants to see either of you ever again after what you did to him…

THE 10 BEST PLAGUES OF MOSES

What Moses did to the Pharaoh is recounted in Exodus 7:14 – 12:34. Quite simply, every time he refused to let the Israelites go, Moses brought a different plague down on him. And was that Pharaoh stubborn! It took 10 plagues to make him give in.

1 The River Nile turned into blood. Not only did this bung up all the taps, it made for a rotten cup of tea.

2 A plague of frogs. Still Pharaoh didn't jump to it and do what Moses asked.

3 Next came a plague of mosquitoes. Moses said to Pharaoh. "You scratch my back and I'll scratch yours," but still he refused.

4 Moses sent gadflies, but still Pharaoh didn't bite.

5 The Egyptians' cattle died. Pharaoh wouldn't moo-ve.

6 Moses sent a fine dust over Egypt which landed on people and made their skin break out in boils. Still Pharaoh said 'No', even though he was bursting to say 'Yes'.

7 A hailstorm flattened most of the Egyptians' crops. It was almost the last straw.

8 A plague of locusts ate all the crops that were standing. This *was* the last straw! But still Pharaoh refused to let the Israelites go.

9 For three days, there was darkness all over the land. Pharaoh didn't know which way to turn.

10 Finally Moses said that every first-born creature – including children – would die. The Israelites marked their door-posts with the blood of a sacrificed lamb so that the Angel of Death would "pass over" them, but every Egyptian first-born died. Among them was the Pharaoh's son.

Compere: What happened then, Aaron?

Aaron: Like, the Pharaoh didn't like the Israelites, like. So he let them go.

Compere: Now, Moses, you lead your people out of Egypt. But little do you know that Pharaoh's changed his mind yet again. He sends his soldiers after you. Just as you reach the Red Sea you see them galloping after you.

Voice off: And what happened next I could not believe.

Compere: He saw the whole thing. Come in Private Abkar of the Egyptian Army.

An old soldier enters.

Compere: So exactly what happened?

Soldier: Well sah, me alarm-dial didn't go off. That made me late starting, so as we got close to the escapees I was still a fair way behind the others. Good job an all, as it turned out! As I get closer I see Moses here stretch his staff out over the water. Wallop! Straight away there's a howling gale blowing! It parted the waves. And before you know it the Israelites are walking across the sea bed! Anyway, they get to the other side. Then I see our lads go across after them. And what happens? The wind drops! The water hasn't got a parting any more. All I can do is stand on the side an watch 'em go under for the third time! That's when I thought: let em go, Abkar, their God's too strong for you. So I turned back.

Compere: Well, Moses. Your people must have been happy after that!

Moses: Nah.

Aaron: All they can do is moan about how much walking they've had to do. So I says to them, "Come on, I mean, best foot forward, eh? Let's play follow the leader." But they're not in the mood. Just in *a* mood. That's when Moses decides there's only one thing to do; have a little meeting with the Boss. And off he goes – for forty days and forty nights!

Loud voice off: Well we had a lot to discuss.

Compere: Moses, you've talked to him every day since that meeting. But you've never actually seen him in person. Now come in, God!

Crashes of thunder, flashes of lightning.

Compere: Unfortunately, you're not going to see him tonight, either. But we've set up a satellite link and you can certainly hear him. Hello, God, are you there?

God: I'm always here.

Compere: So what did you come up with?

God: Remember the covenant I made with Noah, then Abraham? Well, I thought it was time for an update. So that's what I handed down to Moses. Ten easy-to-remember rules…

THE 10 BEST OF ALL TIME
THE 10 COMMANDMENTS (EXODUS 20: 3-17)

1 No other Gods, only ME.
2 Don't make models or idols to worship.
3 No swearing.
4 Must rest on Sundays – no work at all.
5 Respect your Mum and Dad. Do as you're told.
6 No murdering other people.
7 No jumping into bed with somebody who isn't your wife (men), your husband (women) or your hot water bottle (both).
8 No taking anything that belongs to another person.
9 Never accuse innocent people of crimes.
10 No jealousy.

Compere: So, Moses, you came down from the mountain with the 10 Commandments carved on two tablets of stone. And that solved the problems, did it?

Moses: Nah. Made 'em worse.

Aaron: OK, OK. My fault. I made a serious boo-boo. But, come on, put yourself in my position. Forty days Moses had been away. "God can't be in," they said. "We've been tricked. Make us an idol instead." What could I do? They were ready to riot. So I knocked up this golden calf and we had a bit of a party, y'know? More to cheer everybody up than anything else. What happens? Down comes Moses with his new concrete rule-book – and we find we've broken numbers 1, 2, 3 and 7 already!

Compere: And Moses, you smashed the stone tablets on the ground?

Moses: Yeh.

Aaron: Threw a right wobbly, he did. Anyway, off he goes for another forty days and nights before he comes back with another lot. This time it's different, though. We've learned our lesson. We make our own mascot – a big box called the Ark of the Covenant. We put the tablets in it, and from then on that's our mascot.

God: As a sign that I am with them.

Voice off: We won some famous victories on our travels, too.

Compere: Our final guest tonight. Come in, your battle commander – Joshua!

Joshua enters

Joshua: It took a long time. Forty years of battling. But we made it. Canaan's just on the other side of the river.

Moses: Yeh! Yeh! Yeh!

Compere: A wonderful story. So, let's give the final word to God. Almighty, what have you got to say to Moses?

God: Moses, you've done a fine job. Because of you, the Israelites are on the outskirts of the Promised Land. But Moses … at 120 years old, you're not getting any younger. So … I'm sorry, Moses, I've decided to put Joshua in charge.

Moses: What about me? What am I going to do?

God: You're going to join me. In other words, you're going to die. Tonight.

Compere steps forward quickly with his big red book.

Compere: Moses, this *was* your life!

For the Jews, the story of the Exodus is central to their religion for two reasons: first because it's the story of how God saved them from slavery and guided them to the promised land of Israel; and, second because it was on this journey that God gave them the commandments, or laws that he wanted them to obey. Christians also regard the Exodus story as a sign of God at work, mainly because Jesus Christ often referred to different parts of it, especially the 10 Commandments, in his teaching.

BIBLICAL BUT TRIVIAL: NO. 4

Although the route of the Exodus isn't known exactly, the Israelites must have travelled about 805 kilometres (500 miles) in total. As it took them 40 years, that's about 20 kilometres (12½ miles) a year!

FANTASTIC FACTS 4: IT'S THE LAW!

The Ten Commandments were central to the Hebrew faith. Lots of other laws are listed in the Bible, but those 10 mattered the most because they were the latest version of the "covenant" between God and the Hebrew people. In fact, that's why there were *two* tablets of stone. When any agreement was made between two people in those times, each partner kept a copy of the agreement. In the case of the 10 Commandments, one tablet was for the Hebrews to keep and the other for God.

Both copies of the stone tablets were put into the *Ark of the Covenant* and thereafter it was regarded as the "home" of God. Wherever the Hebrews went, the Ark of the Covenant went too. So there was no way that the Israelites could forget the 10 Commandments!

Their influence pops up everywhere in the Old Testament...

1 Thou shalt have no other gods before me.
The Hebrews were told by this commandment to be monotheists: that is, believe in the One God and no others. This was difficult, because all the nations and peoples they mixed with had gods by the dozen.

The story of Phinehas the priest in chapter 25 of the *Book of Numbers* tells of how, during their time in the wilderness, the Israelites started worshipping the gods of the Midianites. As a punishment they were hit by a plague, which killed 24,000 of them – but still they didn't stop. Then, one day, an Israelite brought a Midianite woman right into the Israelite's camp. What did Phinehas do?

Answer:
Took his spear and used it to kill the Midianite woman. The Israelite man died too – because the spear went through him first! The plague was immediately lifted.

2 Thou shalt not make unto thee any graven image… Thou shalt not bow down thyself to them, nor serve them.

The law about not making images was designed to stop the Israelites following the way of religions which were based on worshipping idols – objects and figures which had been made by human hands.

The commandment had some curious effects. One was that you weren't allowed to have tattoos on your body (they were images). But the Ark of the Covenant *was* allowed to be decorated with two gold cherubim, one at either end. Why?

3 Thou shalt not take the name of the Lord thy God in vain.

A name in Old Testament times was thought to reflect
in some way the personality of its owner. That meant
that the name of God was powerful. To use it in a curse,
for instance, was to try to take on the power of God
himself and that was forbidden.

This commandment caused problems. Because God's
name was so special the Israelites reached the stage where
they wouldn't say it aloud, or write it down! So how do
you write somebody's story without mentioning their
name?

Hebrew word "Adonai", meaning Lord. As a reminder, all the Old Testament books were marked up with the vowels of this word.
So what was God's name originally known to the Israelites? Nobody knows! However, it's most likely to have been pronounced "Jahweh" (Yar-way), which means "I am".

4 Remember the Sabbath day, to keep it holy.

Sabbath means "rest", and that's what the Israelites (and their servants, and even their donkeys!) were being commanded to do – rest on one day in seven, just as God did when he created the world. It was to be a day devoted to God. The *Book of Numbers* (15:32-36) tells of a man who was stoned to death for gathering wood on the Sabbath!

5 Honour thy father and thy mother.

This was a much bigger deal than simply eating your greens and going to bed when you were told! It was a deadly serious commandment with, possibly, a deadly serious punishment:

If anyone curses his father or mother, he must be put to death. (Leviticus 20:9)

Commandments 1 – 5 are often grouped together under

the general theme of "You must love the Lord your God". It was God who'd given you to your parents, so by honouring them, you were honouring God too – and by cursing them you were cursing him. So, for how long was the commandment meant to apply?

Answer:
For as long as they lived. It especially meant that you were to care for your parents when they were old and doddery.

6 Thou shalt not kill.

Murder was not allowed. God gave life, and only God was allowed to take it away again. But you *could* chop up your enemies, and people *could* be executed. How come? In both cases the answer is that it was seen as God who was taking the life. Wars fought by the Israelites were "holy wars". God wasn't just on their side, he was fighting with them, so if an enemy's head got cut off it was God who'd done the cutting – he'd just happened to use an Israelite's sword.

In the same way, executions were carried out on people who disobeyed God's laws. The executioner was simply doing it to save God the trouble of firing off a bolt of lightning or whatever.

But what about accidental death? Say you'd caught somebody robbing your house in broad daylight. There'd been a fight and, in the struggle, the crook had been killed. Would you have been considered guilty of murder?

Answer:
The short answer is: Yes. Under the law, your high priest would have had no option but to sentence you to death. Because it was recognized that this was a bit unfair, some special "cities of refuge" were set up. Instead of being executed, you could go to live in one of these instead. For how long? Until the high priest died.

7 Thou shalt not commit adultery.

Commandments 6 – 10 are sometimes grouped under the theme of, "Love your neighbour". But that meant being fair in your dealings with them – not jumping into bed with them! Do that, and you were in big trouble.

If a man and woman were caught together, the penalty was for them both to be stoned to death. For a woman, life wasn't simple even if she was being a faithful wife. If her husband suspected her of seeing another man what could he do?

8 Thou shalt not steal.

So when was stealing, stealing? You're wandering through your neighbour's vineyard. You feel peckish, so you start eating some of his grapes. Are you stealing or not?

Answer:

Only if you took them away. While you were in there you could eat as many of his grapes as you wanted. The grapes were a gift from God to the vineyard owner, and if he's a caring neighbour then he wouldn't mind you munching a few grapes. What you couldn't do, was put a load in a basket and carry them away. That would have been a threat to his livelihood.

The punishment for real theft was very severe, as a man named Gehazi found out. He was the prophet Elisha's servant. When Elisha healed a soldier called Naaman from the skin disease leprosy, Naaman was so grateful he asked Elisha what he wanted as a gift. Elisha refused to take anything.

That's when Gehazi thought of a sneaky plan. He ran after Naaman and told him that Elisha had changed his mind and wanted some silver and two sets of clothes. When Gehazi got back with the stuff he ran straight into Elishah, who was not pleased. Neither was Gehazi when he was told his punishment:

"Naaman's leprosy will cling to you and your descendants for ever." Then Gehazi went from Elisha's presence and he was leprous, as white as snow. (2Kings 5:27)

9 Thou shalt not bear false witness.

Bearing false witness meant more than simply telling lies. Think of a witness in court. It meant trying to get an innocent person convicted of a crime they didn't commit. What was the punishment if you were found out?

97

10 Thou shalt not covet...

To covet means to want something that isn't yours. A famous story in the Old Testament tells of how King Solomon decided a case between two women who both claimed to be the mother of the same baby. How would you have sorted out the case? Here are the details.

- The two women lived in the same house.

- They'd both had babies at the same time.

- They'd both gone to sleep with the babies at their sides.

- But, claimed Woman A, when she woke up, Woman B's baby was by her side and it was dead. Woman B, she said, must have switched the babies after rolling on her own baby and killing it. The living baby was hers.

YOU SWITCHED 'EM YOU SQUASHED YOURS, YA FAT LUMP

I DIDN'T!

- Woman B claimed that Woman A was lying. The dead baby belonged to Woman A. The living baby was hers.

So, what did Solomon say should happen?

Answer:
The baby should be cut in half, with one half going to each woman!

Except that this didn't happen. When Woman A heard Solomon's decision, she pleaded with him to spare the baby's life and give it to Woman B. Woman B, on other hand, told Solomon to get on with it.

Then the king gave his ruling: Give the living baby to the first woman. Do not kill him; she is his mother. (1 Kings 4:16-28)

Solomon knew that the real mother cared so much for her baby that she would rather part with it than see it killed.

Clever stuff!

BIBLICAL AND MIND-BOGGLING: NO. 4

It's thought that the Israelite's miraculous crossing of the Red Sea doesn't refer to the Red Sea in our atlases, but to a crossing at one of its two northern prongs, the Gulf of Aqaba. This is an area of strong winds – strong enough, sometimes, to blow the water away from the usually submerged tip of the Gulf and turn it into dry land!

What happened next...?

For Moses, the journey to Canaan, the Promised Land, ends on the banks of the River Jordan. God tells him that he's not going to go across and into Canaan himself. After seeing it from the top of a mountain as a sort of consolation prize Moses promptly dies.

The Israelites bury Moses and mourn for thirty days. Then they enter Canaan, the land that God originally told Abraham he'd give them way back in history.

There's only one problem. It appears that God hasn't got around to mentioning this to the Canaanites...

STORY 5: JOSHUA
(JOSHUA 1 - 6)

The Israelites had to fight their way into the Promised Land. Fighting battles meant they needed a warrior leader, and Joshua was their man.

He first appears in the Old Testament stories during the various punch-ups the Israelites had during their time in the Wilderness. But it's his promotion to leader in place of Moses that really thrusts him into the limelight. His job is simple: to capture the land of Canaan for the Israelites.

The *Book of Joshua* tells how it was done. As much of it was written hundreds of years after the events described, there's no way that Joshua himself could have been the author. Maybe if he had been, though, this is how it would have looked...

BLOWING MY OWN TRUMPET -

THE WAR MEMOIRS OF JOSHUA

Dateline: 1240 BC

<u>Strategic position</u>: On the banks of the River Jordan.

The top job was mine at last! Real bad luck on Moses, not being around for the final push, but that's life. Or should I say death?

Anyway, imagine the scene. There we were on the banks of the River Jordan. On the other side was the Promised Land — Canaan. Only one problem so far as I can see: somebody's got there before us.

At that moment it seemed a good idea to call God, the supreme Commander. Fortunately, Moses had left me his number in the files. He answered at once.

"How do you get across the river?" he says crisply. "No problem, Josh, my boy. You remember how the red sea parted for old Moses?"

Remember? Who could forget it!

"Yes, Sir," I say. "I was in the first wave of Israelites that went across!"

"Right, we'll get the priests to carry the Ark of the Covenant into the waters of Jordan. The minute they do that, the river will stop flowing."

Talk about making life easy! Why we had to do all those bridge-building and river-wading exercises in training I really don't know.

So, we followed the instructions. And do you know, it worked like a charm! The waters of Jordan stopped moving and we all strolled across.

On we went, to Jericho. This one was a tougher nut to crack.

I'd thought about it before we crossed the river. Jericho was occupied, too. So, how were we going to get them out? As I saw it, there were two options:

① Ask them to leave and hope they didn't say no.

② Kill them all first, then ask them to leave.

Tricky one. So, I decided to find out how the land lay. I wrote out some

103

instructions for a couple of my top spies.

TOP 10 SECRET INSTRUCTIONS

1. Sneak into Jericho and have a look around.
2. Come back and report to me.

3, 4, 5, 6, 7, 8, 9 & 10. DON'T GET CAUGHT!

My two best men were agents Ichibar 001 and Lamechai 002. Funny names, I know, but spying had been in their families for years.

So off they went. All I could do was wait, and a worrying wait it was, too. I had to play my violin to calm my nerves.

Finally, though, the pair of them came back and slapped their report on my desk........

SPY REPORT

We sneaked into Jericho and took rooms in the house of a woman named Rahab. Very reasonable rates (see expense claim attached).

Only one problem — the King had discovered we were there. Maybe we shouldn't have signed the guest book as "001 and 002, spies". Anyway, as Rahab brings us the toast and marmalade next morning she shows us a note she's received.

Dear Rahab,
Those men are spies!
The King.

Luckily, Rahab was on our side. This was probably due to the good tip we left on the table after dinner (see expense claim attached). Anyway, she hides us on the roof (where our best tunics get gnawed by rats — expense claim attached) and sends a note back to the King.

Dear King,
They've escaped!
Rahab

Jolly clever ruse! Off go the King's men while Rahab tells us what's what in Jericho and all that stuff. Apparently the word's got around about your famous victories, Joshua. Everybody there's scared stiff of us. All we have to do is stroll in and take the place. They'll give up at once.

P.S. In return for helping us we had to promise not to butcher Rahab or her family when we take over Jericho. Hope that's O.K.

P.P.S. Don't forget our expenses.

An excellent report. I tore up the expense claims, but agreed to the no-butchering-Rahab-and-co. bit. I'm a merciful chap. Anyway, we were going to have enough on our plate butchering everybody else. So, off we went on a double quick route march. Destination Jericho!

But when we arrived, I saw the full extent of the situation. And it wasn't good. Agents 001 and 002, the cretins had forgotten to mention that the city of Jericho was surrounded by walls that were even thicker than they were.

What to do about it, that was the question. Once again I did what I always did when I needed to think my way through a knotty problem— got out the old violin for a relaxing play. And what do you know, the answer came to me at once. Get on the hot-line to God, of course! No point having a champion on your side and not using him is there?

107

No? It scares me stiff when I hear it, and they're on my side.

No, Joshua! You all stay silent. Not a word. And then you go back to camp.

Er... excuse me, General God. I thought the idea was to capture this place.

It is. I haven't finished yet. Now, the next day you do the same thing again.

A-ha! And this time we sing 'Ere we come, 'ere we come, 'ere we come.

No! You say nothing again, and go back to camp again.

By this time I'm thinking God's got his head in the clouds. Especially when he tells me,

You do this for six days. Then on the seventh day, you get up at dawn and do the same thing. But this time you don't do one lap, you do seven.

Seven?

And that's when you're going to fight.

108

After seven laps! We'll be in no condition to fight anybody! Can't I just play my violin under the King's window? Twenty minutes of that and he'll surrender for sure.

No! Do as I say!

Well, you don't argue with the top brass. So that's what we did. Six laps, one a day, during the week, then seven on the seventh day. Finally we finish.

"Shout men!" I shout.

So everybody shouts. The trumpets sound. And the walls of Jericho just collapse in front of our eyes. It was absolutely amazing.

The rest was a doddle. We walk in, butcher everybody except Rahab, knock the rest of the place down and that's that. Home in time for tea.

Violins — bah! I started trumpet lessons the next day.

So the *Book of Joshua* describes how, with the help of God, the Israelites crossed into Canaan and won their first major battle. It goes on to describe victory after victory, giving the impression that the Israelites swept in and conquered the country in one brilliant campaign.

The Israelites' Unbeaten Run

Although the *Book of Joshua* gives the general impression that the Israelites took over the whole land of Canaan in one go, it wasn't like that at all.

Sometimes they won their battles, but sometimes they lost – and this is the message that runs throughout the Old Testament. If the Israelites obeyed the 10 Commandments and the other laws God had given them, then they always won. But if they'd been up to something naughty, then, they lost.

BIBLICAL BUT TRIVIAL: NO. 5

Mums and dads trying to think of a name for their new baby have been searching the bible for ideas ever since it was written – and they still are.

In 2007, Joshua was the fourth favourite boy's name in Britain and the USA.

FANTASTIC FACTS 5: BLOODTHIRSTY BATTLES

You may be surprised that a holy book like the Bible contains details of bloodthirsty battles, but it does – stacks of them!

This is because it's a *history* book as well as a religious book. It recounts the part played by God in the history of the Hebrews, and their history (just like that of every nation) includes plenty of wars.

Remember what they did: they invaded Canaan in the belief that it was the "Promised Land", the land God had said they could live in forever. But the Canaanites didn't believe in the Hebrew God so they were hardly likely to let them take over without a fight. What's more, even when Israel was established that wasn't the end of the matter. The Israelites fought battles with the Canaanites who wanted to get their land back, and they also fought other peoples who wanted to invade the land just as the Israelites had done. Sometimes, the Israelites even fought battles against each other!

So, if you're squeamish, turn quickly to the next story. If not, read on for the 10 Best facts about bloodthirsty Biblical battling!

1 To fight or not to fight?

The first question any Israelite leader would have to ask was: Is it right to fight? There was one condition that always had to be satisfied, and that wasn't anything like: Have we got as many men as the other side? It was: Does God want us to fight?

The Israelites went up and wept before the Lord until evening, and they enquired of the Lord. They said, "Shall we go up again to battle...?"

The Lord answered, "Go up against them." (Judges 20: 23)

These pre-fight chats with God were either handled by the leaders, like Moses or Joshua, or in later times by the priests. If God said, "Do not fight," then for the Israelite commander it was bad news. If he went ahead and fought the battle it would be his fault if they lost. But if God said, "go for it", then the Israelites fought whether they were outnumbered or not...

2 Holy battles!

In this way, every battle the Israelites fought was a "holy" battle. God didn't just want them to fight, he was on their side. The Ark of the Covenant would be set up in a special tent (or tabernacle) as a sign that God was actually with them in their camp.

This must have made life uncomfortable. Nothing unclean could be anywhere near God's presence. So the loos had to be outside the camp!

God's rules of battle were pretty straightforward.

When you march up to attack a city, make its people an offer of peace. If they accept and open their gates, all the people in it shall ... work for you (Deuteronomy 21:10)

Not surprisingly, the Israelites' opponents didn't always accept their kind offer. When that happened, the battle was on!

3 Strong-arm stuff!

As far as the Israelites were concerned, when the fighting began God didn't stay back in the camp. He was there, fighting alongside them. Sometimes, as in the siege of Jericho, the Ark of the Covenant was carried into battle as a sign of this.

As to *how* God helped, the Old Testament writers give plenty of examples. One of the earliest took place when Moses was leading the Israelites through the wilderness and, with Joshua in command, they fought a battle against a bunch known as the Amalekites. Moses had a staff that God had endowed with special powers. So, during the battle, Moses kept the staff held high. While he did that, the Israelites were winning. The trouble was, even Moses couldn't keep his arms up in the air all day – and when he lowered them the Amalekites started winning. So...

They took a stone and put it under him and he sat on it. Aaron and Hur held his hands up – one on one side, one on the other – so that his hands remained steady till sunset. So Joshua overcame the Amalekite… (Exodus 17:10-13)

That's what you call an arm-y!

I'M SLIPPING! GIVE US A HAND!

4 Ai, Ai! Where have they gone?

God wasn't only in there fighting. He dictated tactics as well. The Book of Joshua tells the story of how, after capturing Jericho, Joshua went on to tackle another city named Ai.

Then the Lord said to Joshua… "Set an ambush behind the city." (Joshua 8:4)

Joshua, sensible chap, did as he was told. He led some men up to the city gates then, when the Ai-ites came out after them, ran away. That allowed the 30,000 men he'd hidden in the bushes at the rear of the city the previous night to jump out and capture Ai without any trouble!

YOU WEREN'T EXPECTING THIS, WERE YOU??!!!

5 It never rains…

Sometimes, God even joined in the fighting! As word of Joshua's victories spread, the king of a people called the

Gibeonites decided that he didn't fancy fighting such a powerful army. He made a peace treaty with Joshua.

Other kings thought this was like joining forces with the enemy so they promptly attacked the Gibeonites to teach them a lesson. The Israelites joined the battle in defence of their new friends – and so did God! When Joshua and his troops attacked...

The Lord hurled large hailstones down on them from the sky, and more of them died from the hailstones than were killed by the swords of the Israelites. (Joshua 10:10)

NASTY WEATHER FOR THIS TIME OF YEAR, DON'T YOU THINK?

6 A sticky business

The *Book of Judges* tells of life after Joshua, and of the battles fought by the Israelites under a succession of warrior leaders called "Judges". One of them was named Barak.

By then the leader wasn't always the one who did the talking with God. A prophetess named Deborah did this, on behalf of Barak, before a battle against a Canaan army that was equipped with the latest line in iron chariots. However the story was still the same, except that this time God told Deborah where Barak was to hold the battle: near the River Kishon. When the battle was fought, the enemy abandoned their chariots (presumably because they got stuck in the mud) and...

The River Kishon swept them away... (Judges 5:21)

7 Unfair sides!

Even being outnumbered didn't matter. In fact on one occasion, God was supposed to have reduced the size of the Israelite army, just to make it clear that it was his power that would lead to the victory, not the Israelites' fighting ability!

This happened in a battle against a people called the Midianites. Another warrior named Gideon set out for the battle with an army of 32,000 men. God made Gideon send all but 300 of them away! What's more, each of them was told to carry a trumpet, a torch and an empty jug – but no sword!

Why? Obvious! They crept up to the Midianite camp at night, hiding their torches in the empty jugs. When they got there, they smashed the jugs and started blowing their trumpets and hollering. All the dozy Midianites jumped out of bed and…

The Lord caused the men throughout the camp to turn on each other with their swords. (Judges 8:22)

Yes, the Midianites started fighting each other. All Gideon's men had to do was catch the few survivors.

8 Ban the lot

If the inhabitants of a captured city weren't worshippers of God, the "Do not kill and do not steal" didn't apply. Quite the opposite. If it was a far-away city then they had to kill all the men; the women, children and animals they could keep for themselves. If it was a city in the land of Canaan, though, they were told...

Do not leave alive anything that breathes. Completely destroy them. Otherwise they will teach you to follow all the detestable things they do... (Deuteronomy 21:16-18)

9 Gotcha!

Men tended to get butchered whenever they lost in a battle, simply so that they couldn't fight again. If you were a king it could be even worse; you could be tortured to death, then nailed up on a tree as a warning to other kings not to try the same trick. Women and children were luckier. If they were captured, they became the Israelites' slaves.

One Canaanite king got double treatment. His name was Adoni-Bezek, and he'd been in the habit of doing nasty things to the kings that he beat, before making them into his slaves. When he was beaten by the Israelites he received a taste of his own medicine:

They chased him and caught him and cut off his thumbs and big toes. Then Adoni-Bezek said, "Seventy kings with

117

their thumbs and big toes cut off have picked up scraps under my table. Now God has paid me back for what I did to them." (Judges 1:6)

10 The final battle

There are hundreds more battles mentioned in the Old Testament. Some the Israelites won, some they lost. In the latter part of the period they lost many more than they won. This, according to the writers, was because they'd stopped worshipping God and he'd abandoned them.

Slowly, the idea developed that one day a special leader for Israel would be born. He (and it was definitely going to be a man) would finally lead them to freedom, after which they'd live in peace forever. The Hebrew word for this man was "Messiah".

For unto us a child is born, to us a son is given, and the government will be on his shoulders. And he will be called Wonderful Counsellor, Mighty God, Everlasting Father, Prince of Peace. (Isaiah 9:6)

Christians believe that this child was born in Bethlehem; that the Messiah predicted in the Old Testament finally came in the person of Jesus Christ. Jews don't believe this; they are still waiting for the Messiah.

BIBLICAL AND MIND-BOGGLING: NO. 5

There have been a number of cities of Jericho. The one dating closest to the time of Joshua was surrounded by two walls. Its inner wall was 3.65 metres thick; the outer wall was 1.83 metres thick and over 9 metres high.

Although there's no proof that Joshua's army was responsible, archaeologists have discovered that these walls didn't crumble away, but were squashed flat in one go!

What happened next...

One way or another, the Israelites captured large lumps of Canaan. They then, according to the *Book of Joshua*, held a big meeting to decide how the territory was to be divided up.

The Canaan carve-up

The result was that different areas of Canaan were allocated to each of the twelve "tribes" of Israel. What were the names of these tribes? You may recognise ten of them: Reuben, Simeon, Judah, Issachar, Zebulun, Dan, Naphtali, Gad, Asher and Benjamin – yes, ten of the sons of Jacob. The two missing sons are Joseph and Levi, but they're both accounted for.

The Levi became the priests – the holy men – of Israel. They were expected to wander around, running the religious side of things for all the tribes, and didn't get any land to call their own. But there was a rule that any tribe had to give the Levites somewhere to live whenever they needed it.

119

As for top dog Joseph, he's only left out because his family gets double shares. The final two tribes are Manasseh and Ephraim, named after Joseph's own two sons.

So, did the Joseph story really happen – or was it just a way of explaining how the tribes came in to being?

Next, please!
Whacked out with all the fighting and dividing, Joshua dies. Who takes his place as leader? Nobody.

Having got their land, the tribes go off and do their own thing – and, as the Old Testament so often says, that isn't always the thing that God wants them to do. The result? Trouble, usually in the shape of punch-ups with nations on their borders.

Come in… The Judges!

STORY 6: SAMSON AND DELILAH (JUDGES 13 - 16)

The Judges were individual heroes, often leading one particular tribe in a fight with another nation – and there were plenty of other nations to fight with!

As the *Book of Judges* makes clear, there were large areas of Canaan that the Israelites hadn't taken over. Not surprisingly the people living in those areas often decided they weren't going to wait around to be captured, so they started a fight with Israel first.

As far as the Old Testament writers were concerned, this would always happen when one of the tribes wasn't being good and keeping to the Covenant that God had made with it. In other words, if any Israelites got beaten up it was because God was allowing it to happen as a punishment.

But eventually, God would raise up a "judge" to come to the rescue. Forget about the judges you see nowadays, in robes and wigs. These were a much rougher bunch. The judges of the Old Testament didn't sit on benches, they picked them up and thumped opponents with them. They were military leaders who became heroes because of **the way they fought opposing nations.**

One particular nation was particularly feared. The people were known as the Philistines, and they inhabited the western coastal part of Canaan.

The Israelites versus The Philistines was on "Battle of the Day" more times than any other contest. And so the judge who fought them had to be a very strong character indeed...

Sam's the man

His name was Samson. He was a Nazirite – that is, a person who had dedicated a period of his life to God. As a sign of this, Samson never cut his hair. In return, God gave him: immense strength, a powerful temper and no brains. For a start, he married a Philistine! Pretty dumb, when you're

SAMSON

supposed to be their bitter enemy. Off he goes to visit his wife, only to find that his father-in-law has given her away to one of Samson's friends.

Powerful temper working powerfully, Samson catches 300 foxes, ties their tails together in pairs and puts torches in the knots. Then he sets the foxes loose in the Philistine cornfields to burn their crops. To pay Samson back, the Philistines murder his wife.

A bit of an ass

Samson runs off and hides in a cave in the Judaean area of Canaan. Three thousand Judaeans promptly come looking for him, moaning that the Philistines (their rulers) are giving them a hard time because of what Samson has done. They tie him up and take him back.

Time for some immense strength. As he's brought to the Philistines, Samson breaks free. Picking up the jawbone of a donkey that just happens to be lying around he defends himself. A few minutes and a thousand dead Philistines later, the fight was over.

In spite of everything, Samson finds another Philistine girlfriend. This one's named Delilah, and she turns out to be the biggest trouble of the lot...

DELIGHTFUL DELILAH

The various stories about Samson are assumed to be folk tales which have been retold by the Old Testament writers to show the hatred between the Israelites and the Philistines at this time.

Even so, Samson's story had a serious message. It was the usual one: stick with God, and you're OK. Leave him, and you're in trouble! Samson had promised to devote his life to God – and showed this by not cutting his hair. When he allows his hair to be cut, it's as though he's broken his promise – his strength didn't come from his hair but from God. Only when Samson comes back to God (his hair growing again shows he's had plenty of time in prison to think about it!) does his strength return.

BIBLICAL BUT TRIVIAL: NO. 6

If you want to insult somebody (not your teacher – at least, not within earshot) call them a "Philistine". Today it means "ill-behaved and ignorant"!

FANTASTIC FACTS 6: PLAYING THE SYMBOLS

The length of Samson's hair was symbolic – a sign (and not just of the fact that he didn't go to the barbers).

It showed that he was a Nazirite, a man who had dedicated a period of his life to God. At the end of that period his hair would be shaved off and burnt. This was another symbol – the smoke produced wafted upwards into the heavens, to where God was.

The Bible is jam-packed with symbols. Here's a quiz about 10 of the best.

1 Food and drink
Common food items are often used as symbols in the Old Testament. Probably the most famous pair are used by God to describe the Promised Land:

I have indeed seen the misery of my people in Egypt... So I have come down to rescue them ... and to bring them up out of that land into ... a land flowing with...
(Exodus 4:7-8)

Flowing with what?

Answer:
Milk and honey.

Put this combination on the menu for school dinners and it probably wouldn't get too many takers. But for the Israelites milk and honey meant something great. They didn't drink tea or coffee, but drank lots of milk which they got for free from their goats and cattle. Wild honey was free too, deposited by bees in rocks, trees and other places, and it might be the difference between life and death for somebody wandering in the desert. A land flowing with milk and honey, meant a land of plenty.

2 Trees and plants

Grandparents nowadays have a habit of saying daft things like, "Haven't you grown! I remember when you were knee high to a grasshopper!" (Even though grasshoppers don't have knees!) But what might Old Testament grandparents have compared you to?

Answer:

A tree, in particular a cedar. This was a common image for somebody growing, not just on the outside, but inside in their devotion to God.

The righteous will flourish like a palm tree, they will grow like the cedar of Lebanon. (Psalm 92:12)

As a cedar tree can grow to 30m (100ft) high, and almost as wide, you can see it was a powerful symbol.

3 Oil

No, not the stuff you put on your bike chain, but the stuff you get from fruits like the olive. For the Old Testament peoples it was used for everything from a medicine to a fuel, from keeping hair smooth to use in religious services as "holy oil".

The practice still goes on today. Oil was used during the Coronation of Queen Elizabeth II for exactly the same reason as during Old Testament times. What for, and why?

Answer:

Oil is put on the head of a new king or queen as a sign that God has crowned them to act on his behalf on earth.

The oil is a symbol of God's power. In the Old Testament, anything connected with God was "anointed" – that is it had oil rubbed on it. This amounted to everything from furniture (like the Ark of the Covenant) to the heads of kings and priests.

Zadok the priest took the horn of oil... and anointed Solomon. Then they sounded the trumpet and all the people shouted, "Long live King Solomon!" (1 Kings 1:39)

(Queen Elizabeth got trumpets and "Long live the Queen!")

4 Water

Water represented four things for the Israelites:

birth: because God's spirit had hovered over the waters in order to create the earth

fertility: because water was necessary to make anything grow

danger: water was powerful enough to kill (ask the Egyptian soldiers who'd chased after Moses!)

and... what?

Answer:

Cleanliness. Yes, the Israelites were very keen on washing! Not just because it got the dirt off, but because it was a symbol of being pure. A soldier who'd been out fighting the enemy had become "unclean" by touching them (even if he'd only touched them with the end of his sword). When he came back to camp, where God was living, he had to stay outside for seven days. Then:

On the seventh day wash your clothes and you will be clean. Then you may come into the camp. (Numbers 31:24)

5 Numbers

Here's a riddle for your maths teacher. When is a number not a number? Answer: when it's in the Old Testament, because then it's often a symbol.

Here's a Top 10 countdown, of some really special numbers:

10 Seventy meant "a lot" (seventy descendants of Jacob moved to Egypt to live with Joseph). As for seventy multiplied by anything, that could only mean "more than enough" – which may be why King Solomon was said to have had seven hundred wives!

9 Forty years was taken to be a fixed, but long, period of time. The Israelites were in the wilderness for forty years; all the best kings reigned for forty years. King David was doubly good:

David was thirty years old when he became King and reigned for forty years. (Samuel 5:4)

8 Thirty represented the age of maturity. Joseph was said to be that age when he started working for the Pharaoh.

7 Twelve is a number of completeness, like seven. The Old Testament always talks of the twelve tribes as representing all Israel. One of the stops on the Israelites'

journey to the Promised Land was at Elim where there were twelve springs (*Numbers 33:9*) that is, a perfect spot for water.

6 Ten was simply a nice round number. It was used, along with hundreds and thousands (multiples of ten). So when we're told that Samson *struck down a thousand men* (*Judges 16:15*), it may not have been *exactly* one thousand – but it was a lot!

5 Seven was the number of the day when God rested after the creation. It was symbolic of completion or perfection. The seventh day was the holy day, the Sabbath. All the great festivals lasted seven days. Hebrew slaves would dream of their seventh year – because then they were allowed to go free!

4 Five being the number of fingers on one hand, was used to represent a few – yes, a "handful"! Similarly, five hundred meant a few hundred.

3 Four represented the world. There are four seasons and, for the Old Testament people, four kinds of living creatures: humans, domestic animals, wild animals, and creatures of the sky and sea.

2 Three and a half was often used to indicate a period of time that was under the control of God. A drought in the time of the "wicked" King Ahab was thought to have lasted three and a half years.

1 Three is thought of as a special number in a lot of religions. Anything that the Israelites saw as the work of God was said to have taken three days. For example, Joshua told the Israelites before they entered the Promised Land:

Get your supplies ready. Three days from now you will cross the Jordan and go in and take possession of the land the Lord your God is giving you for your own. (Joshua 1:10)

6 Clothes

What you wore could also be symbolic. Somebody in mourning would cover themselves in sackcloth, a cloth made out of goat's hair. The mourning needn't be because a relative had died. It could be because you had "died" symbolically – that is, done something bad that had made you unworthy to God.

If that was the case, what would you have done with your normal clothes?

Answer:

Torn them up. Tearing your clothes was a sign of great distress. When Joshua was defeated at Ai and realized that somebody must have done something to displease God he:

Tore his clothes and fell face down to the ground before the Ark of the Lord, remaining there until evening. (Joshua 7:6)

It may not be a good idea to do this if your parents tell you off!

7 Gestures

In your school, do you stand up when a teacher (or maybe just the headteacher) enters the room? If so, then you're using a symbolic gesture. Standing up is a sign of respect. What did the Israelites do?

Answer:

Rise in the presence of the aged, show respect for the elderly. (Leviticus 19:32)

In other words – stand up. That's probably why you do it (especially if your teachers are aged and elderly!) But what about if you wanted to show contempt – that is, the opposite of respect? Then you used a different symbolic gesture, such as the locals did to Job after he'd lost everything (seen as God abandoning him):

They detest me and keep their distance; they do not hesitate to spit in my face. (Job 30:10)

They must have been powerful shots if they could keep their distance *and* spit in his face, but you get the idea!

8 Marriage

Yes, marriage was symbolic too. The Old Testament writers used the picture of a husband and wife living together as a symbol of God and the people of Israel. God was the bridegroom, and Israel the bride. But was it shown as a happy or unhappy marriage?

Answer:

Both. A happy marriage was shown as the ideal, with the Israelites obeying God and living happily with him as a wife would obey her husband in a good marriage. This was usually followed by a clear picture of where the Israelites had got it wrong! Worshipping other gods was the same as leaving a husband to go off with another man...

Like a woman unfaithful to her husband, so you have been unfaithful to me, O house of Israel, says the Lord. (Jeremiah 3:20)

But God was always shown as being ready to take his

wife back again – so long as she changed her ways...

I will betroth you to me for ever... in love and compassion. I will betroth you in faithfulness, and you will acknowledge the Lord. (Hosea 2:19-20)

9 Death

As well as wearing sackcloth, a person in mourning would often sprinkle ashes or dust on themselves. Why?

Answer:

Because dust and ashes symbolized death. According to the Book of Genesis, Adam had been created from the soil. When he and Eve disobeyed God, the severest penalty they received was that they were no longer immortal: they would die one day.

For dust you are and to dust you will return. (Genesis 3:19) The same symbol is used when somebody is buried nowadays. The words: "dust to dust, ashes to ashes" will be spoken, as some soil is sprinkled on the coffin.

10 Names

Names really meant something in Old Testament days. Virtually every Hebrew name had a meaning. Place names described the place itself. Horeb, the place in the wilderness where the Ten Commandments were received means "dry". Eden means "pleasant".

So it was with the names of people. The Old Testament writers used names in the same way: Jacob, for example, means "he takes the place of" – perfect for the man who tricked his brother Esau into letting him take his place as heir.

So parents would try hard to find the most suitable name for their child. Perhaps you've got an Old Testament name? Something like Mahershalalhashbaz, perhaps, or Tilgathpilneser? These names have fallen by the wayside (thank goodness!) but there are still plenty of other Old Testament names in regular use today.

So, try this 10 Best selection of names. Can you match the name with its meaning?

1 Rebecca
2 Judith
3 Naomi
4 Miriam
5 Esther
6 Adam
7 Joseph
8 Daniel
9 Joshua
10 Benjamin

A Human
B God is my judge
C A star
D A rope with a noose
E Obstinacy, rebellion
F May God give increase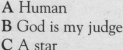
G Son of the right hand
H God is salvation
I Pleasant
J Praiseworthy

Answers:

1 – D (Not as bad as it sounds – it implied that the girl was so beautiful she could capture boys with no trouble!); 2 – J; 3 – I; 4 – E; 5 – C; 6 – A; 7 – F; 8 – B; 9 – H; 10 – G (that is, happiness!)

BIBLICAL AND MIND-BOGGLING: NO. 6

The Philistines were Israel's bitter enemies. Their aim was to destroy the Israelite nation completely, but they failed. Eventually they vanished as a nation and were absorbed by Israel. Worse, by then the name of Israel's land had also changed. It was no longer called Canaan, but Palestine – a name derived from Philistine.

What happened next?

Despite all the triumphs of the Judges, the Israelites' enemies were still thick on the ground. In particular, the Philistines were getting stronger and stronger.

Realising that they were going to have real trouble if they didn't do something drastic, the tribes of Israel decided to get themselves a bit more organised. Instead of fighting individual battles they all got together for the first time since the Exodus and agreed to support each other.

As a sign of this togetherness, they also decided they wanted a king like all the other nations. Fair enough, you might think, but actually this was bad news. God was supposed to be their undisputed leader; wanting a king was a sign that the people didn't trust God to sort things out for them any more.

Even so, God agreed to let them have it their own way. A prophet named Samuel was packed off to find them a king. He hunted around and came up with a man named Saul.

But no sooner had Saul been anointed king, than along came the Philistines again. And this time they were looking for trouble in a BIG way...

STORY 7: DAVID AND GOLIATH (1 SAMUEL 17:1-54)

The Philistines wanted to take over parts of Israel again. They'd obviously decided that the land they had wasn't big enough – and, if the size of at least one of their soldiers is to be believed, it's no wonder why!

Goliath was a *big* hero, the Philistine's champion. Compared to him, the Israelite's biggest soldiers looked puny. And David, a shepherd boy and a part-time harp-player in King Saul's court looked puny compared to them. So how would a straight fight between David and Goliath turn out?

The first Book of Samuel tells the story. But here's how the newspapers might have handled it if they'd been around in 1000 BC...

THE BIG BATTLE BY GOLLY!
GOLIATH CHALLENGE SENSATION

There was no fighting at all today in the battle between the Israelites and the Philistines. But it doesn't mean peace. Far from it! In a sensational new development, Goliath the Philistine marched into the centre of the pitch and threw out a dramatic challenge:

"Us Philistines don't want to mess about playing one of these 10,000 a side battles. They take far too long that way. So I challenge you Israelites to put up one of your team against me in single combat. As the rules say, if he beats me... ho-ho-ho... then you Israelites win and we'll be your slaves; but if I smash him to pulp then you've got to be our slaves. Right?"

And with that, he marched off the field again, laughing loudly.

BUT WILL GOLIATH HAVE THE LAST LAUGH?

The umpires had a look at the rules, and it seems Goliath is perfectly correct. A battle can be decided by one player from each side. They've given King Saul 24 hours to name his player.

BIG BATTLE EXCLUSIVE INTERVIEW WITH KING SAUL

At a hastily convened press conference, our correspondent asks King Saul the questions you, our readers, want answered.

SAUL ANSWERS OUR CALL!

Q: King Saul, can you tell us the latest news? Have you found a challenger to face Goliath?

King Saul: Er… what I can say is that I've just held a meeting with my cabinet on this very matter.

Q: And did you get any volunteers?

King Saul: No, the cabinet didn't answer. Neither did the armchair or the standard lamp.

Q: But what about your soldiers?

King Saul: None of them turned up. In fact, nobody turned up. That's why I was talking to my cabinet…

BIG BATTLE SPECIAL
DAVE'S OUR BOY

Israel has found a challenger to fight Goliath! Just as King Saul was getting desperate and thinking he might have to take on the phorceful Philistine himself, in walked a volunteer. Wait for it, though. He's no soldier. His name is David – and he's a shepherd boy!

So you can forget the Big Fight. This is being billed as the Big v Little Fight!

"OK," said King Saul at another hastily convened press conference today, "So David's a bit on the small side – well, a bit small on all sides to be honest – but he's a keen, enthusiastic lad. Yes, he's an unknown.

CAN DARING DAVID FLATTEN THE PHILISTINE?

Half his flock wouldn't recognise him in the field, and the other half think he's baa-king mad. But he pleaded to be selected. So, I agreed. OK, he'll be the underdog, but he could just spring a surprise."

"Do you think he will?" the King was asked.

"Nope."

FIGHTERS' FACT FILES

Here's how the two contenders shape up for tomorrow's big battle!

DAVID

From: Up the road and it's the 2nd sheep field on the left

Jobs:
* part-time shepherd boy
* part-time armour-carrier for King Saul

Height: Not much

Weight: Not much either

Hobbies: Playing the harp. Writing poems

Favourite Weapon: Sling-shot

Manager: God.

GOLIATH

From: Gath

Job:
Full-time soldier in the
Philistine Army (Attack and
Annihilate Department)

Height: 6 cubits and a span 3
metres (9ft 9ins)

Weight: Not known, but
his breastplate weighs 5000
sheckels (65 Kgs)

Hobbies: Killing Israelites

Favourite Weapons: Big, heavy javelin; bigger, heavier,
sword; even bigger, even heavier, spear (7.8Kgs)

Manager: Not God.

MEET THE CONTESTANTS

Find out how the two contestants in the Big Battle
think it's going to go.

Who will win – Gigantic Goliath, or Diddy David?

Q: Goliath, you've been the champ for a number of years
now. Is it tough at the top?

Goliath: Nah. A bit cold, but when you're as tall as me
that's the way it is.

Q: And how do you think the fight will go?

Goliath: Pretty much the same as always. I'll flatten him, then I'll tear him limb from limb. Then I'll feed the little tweet's body to the birds.

Q: You don't expect this fight to last long, then?

Goliath: None of my fights have lasted longer than five seconds. I reckon this one might take a little longer.

Q: Because you think David will be a tougher opponent?

Goliath: Nah! Because he's such a titch it'll take me a while to spot him!

Q: David, nobody is giving you much of a chance. What exactly is your big fight record?

David: Against people? Er… this will be my first contest.

Q: Your first! You've never fought before?

David: No, no, I didn't say that! I've fought before, but only against lions and bears who've tried to steal one of my lambs.

Q: But surely Goliath is going to be a tougher prospect?

David: No, he'll be pretty much the same. A big pussy cat who'll be grizzly at the end.

Q: You really think you'll win? Goliath says he's going to feed your body to the birds.

David: Well I'm going to feed his body to the birds, so there! And I'm going to cut his head off and that'll show him, won't it!

Q: One last question. Your manager, God. What influence has he had on your career?

David: He's taught me all I know. I'm going to dedicate this fight to him.

146

BIG FIGHT RESULT
WHAT A GREAT DAY-VID!
UNDERDOG SLAYS GIANT

by I Stillcantbelieveit

David, the biggest (or littlest) outsider in Big Fight history, confounded

GOLIATH STOOD A MERE STONES THROW FROM DAVID!

all the experts yesterday and beat the Philistine champion, Goliath.

And it was all over in seconds.

As the signal was given, Goliath moved forward. He was looking really mean and ugly.

From the other side of the battle field, David moved forward. He was looking really hard. What for we all wondered?

We soon found out, as he bent down and picked up a round pebble and put it in his pouch. "First round to David!" shouted somebody. Then we watched as the boy picked up another four pebbles. What was he planning to do with them?

By now, Goliath was clanking in his direction and bellowing something about the only stone David was going to need was a gravestone.

But the little chap took no notice. Pulling out his sling-shot, he popped one of the stones into it. He whirled it round his head a few times – then fired!

Goliath never saw it coming, even though it hit him right between the eyes. The Philistine champion toppled forward, his skull broken. A first round knock-out! As he'd promised, David then cut Goliath's head off with the giant's own giant sword to make it into a first round knock-off as well!

So, the Israelites have a new champion. Watch this boy, that's my advice. He's going to get ahead – unlike Goliath.

"HEADS I WIN!" CRIES A TRIUMPHANT DAVID!!!!

BIBLICAL BUT TRIVIAL: NO. 7

This story has passed into everyday use – even onto the sports pages of the newspapers! When a non-league side take on a premiership team in the FA cup for instance, it's regularly called a "David and Goliath" contest.

FANTASTIC FACTS 7:
LET US PRAY

During his reign as king, David did a lot of good things – and a lot of bad things too. One of the best, as far as the Old Testament writers were concerned, was his decision to build a temple in Jerusalem as the centre for worshipping God and housing the Ark of the Covenant.

It was started by David and completed by his son, Solomon. From then on, it was the place that all Hebrews had to try to get to at least once a year (and faithful Jews still have the same aim today).

Here's a Top Ten fact file on Hebrew worship.

1 The Passover
The Passover, was a major festival. In later years the ideal was to celebrate The Passover in Jerusalem, but for many years it was celebrated in the home.

It was an important ceremony, because it commemorated the Hebrews' escape from Egypt and, in particular, from the tenth plague which God sent to finally convince the rotten Pharaoh it was time to let them go. This plague was the one which killed off every first-born male in the land, including the Pharaoh's son. It "passed over" the Hebrew families because God told them to:

Take a lamb ... slaughter them at twilight ... take some of the blood and put it on the sides and tops of the door-frames. On that same night I will pass through Egypt and strike down every firstborn ... when I see the blood I will pass over you... (Exodus 12:3-13)

The passover ceremony, then, involved eating a meal of cooked lamb. But, in addition, the Hebrews had to follow what their ancestors had done on that night and eat it with unleavened bread (bread made quickly, without yeast) and bitter herbs. They also had to eat this meal standing up and dressed in their outdoor clothes. Why? Because it symbolised how their ancestors had eaten it – all ready to make a run for it!

2. The Ark of the Covenant

The Ark, as we've already seen, was made on the Exodus journey to hold the stone tablets of the Ten Commandments. It had two other things in it as well: a pot of manna, and the branch of a tree! Both of these were collected on the same journey.

The manna arrived when the Israelites were starving. Good old Moses told God about the problem. Sure enough next morning...

Thin flakes of frost appeared on the desert floor. When the Israelites saw it they said to each other, "What is it?"... Moses said to them, It is the bread the Lord has given you to eat." (Exodus 16:14-15)

Further supplies turned up every day, and the Israelites didn't starve. (The phrase is still used today; an unexpected bonus which gets you out of a hole is called "manna from heaven".)

The tree branch belonged to Aaron, Moses' brother. On another occasion when the Israelites were grumbling, God had convinced them that Aaron was his choice as high priest by having Moses collect a staff from the leader of each of the twelve tribes (Aaron was of the tribe of Levi), put their names on them, and then leave them overnight in the same tent as the Ark of the Covenant. Next morning, the sign that Aaron was the chosen priest of God was amazingly clear:

Aaron's staff … had not only sprouted but had budded, blossomed and had produced almonds (Numbers 17:7-8)

A nutty story? Maybe, but for the Israelites Aaron's staff plus the manna and the tablets of the 10 Commandments were signs of God's work. That made the Ark holy, and the central sign of God's presence.

3 The Feast of Tabernacles

This was a feast held in the autumn when the crops had been gathered. The "tabernacle" part of the name comes about because as part of the celebration the people would make tents and camp outside.

It was to symbolize that on their 40-year trek to the Promised Land the Israelites had lived in tents. Celebrating this feast was a reminder of that time, and a thanksgiving that it was over. Needless to say, it was a good bash. Everybody enjoyed themselves – because the scriptures told them to:

Celebrate the Feast of Tabernacles for seven days after you have gathered the produce of your threshing-floor and your winepress. Be joyful... (Deuteronomy 16:13)

4 High Places

Where did regular worship take place? Often in houses, but for major celebrations the Israelites would head off to somewhere special (perhaps in the way people head off to a church today). In the case of an Israelite, it was "a high place".

A high place was just that: the top of a hill, or even a mountain. These were the best places to worship because they were closer to the heavens, which meant they were closer to God. Remember Moses picked up the Ten Commandments after meeting God at the top of Mount Horeb.

At the top of the high place was an altar. You can tell what the altar was for from the meaning of the Hebrew equivalent, which means "slaughtering place". Yes, it was where the animal sacrifices were carried out. The poor creature was popped on the altar to be killed.

Before the Temple of Jerusalem was built, high places were everywhere. Afterwards, Jerusalem was the only place an Israelite was allowed to sacrifice to God. In part this was also because the people had started using the high places to join in with the idol-worship of their Canaan neighbours. So the high places became no-go areas or, more accurately, "get lost" areas. Prophets told the people that such places had to be destroyed – and they didn't mince their words:

This is what the sovereign Lord says:...I am about to bring a sword against you, and I will destroy your high places. Your altars will be...smashed and I will slay your people...I will scatter your bones around your altars. (Ezekiel 6:3-6)

5 Priests

A priest was a middle-man who offered sacrifices on behalf of the common people. No, not to save them from having to do the sacrificing themselves, but because priests were believed to have been specially chosen by God. If a king wanted to know what God was thinking, then he asked the priest to find out.

And, alternatively, if God wanted to tell the people he was chuffed with them, then he told a priest to pass on the good news in the form of a blessing:

The Lord said to Moses, "Tell Aaron and his sons... This is how you are to bless the Israelites. Say to them: "The Lord bless you and keep you. The Lord make his face shine upon you and be gracious to you; the Lord turn his face towards you and give you peace." (Numbers 6:22-26)

Those words are still used as a blessing within Judaism and Christianity.

6 The Jerusalem Temple

The Temple was actually built by David's son, Solomon. It wasn't big, but it was certainly luxurious! It measured about 30ft x 87ft (9m x 27m) – slightly longer than a tennis court, but not quite as wide. Inside were three rooms (three was a holy number, remember!).

The first was the porch, which was reached by passing between two huge pillars. The pillars had names! They were called Jachin ("he makes") and Boaz, ("strength") meaning something like "together he makes us strong".

The second room was known as the "holy place" and contained, amongst other things, a table for "showbread" – twelve loaves, one for each tribe of Israel, given as an offering every sabbath.

The third room was the most important of the lot. Its walls were overlaid with pure gold. It was called the "Holy of Holies" and it contained – nothing...

7 The Ark of the Covenant – II

Well, not at first. The Holy of Holies was where the Ark of the Covenant was to be placed. The only trouble was that by the time it was being built, the Ark had been lost. It had been captured in a battle some years before with David's old pals...

The Philistines fought, and the Israelites were defeated and ... the slaughter was very great; Israel lost thirty thousand foot soldiers. The Ark of God was captured.
(1Samuel 4:10-11)

But it hadn't been destroyed. Believing it to be a powerful object, the Philistines had put it in one of their own temples – only to find their people dying by the dozen. So they moved it to another place, then another. But everywhere it went, death and destruction followed. Finally, and not surprisingly, they wanted to see the back of it.

So they gave it to a Hebrew named Abinabad, whose son looked after it in his house for twenty years! Finally it was brought to Jerusalem by David and put in a temporary tabernacle until the temple was built.

8 The Psalms

What kind of prayers did the Hebrews say? To answer this, go to the section of the Old Testament known as the Book of Psalms. This is a collection of "poems" (but don't look for any rhymes!) which were used in a variety of different circumstances.

If it had been a good day, you praised God:

Praise the Lord, O my soul. O Lord my God, you are very great... (Psalm 104: 1-2)

If you'd had a problem solved, then you gave thanks:

I call to the Lord ... and I am saved from my enemies... (Psalm 18: 3)

And if you'd got a problem which was all your fault and you knew it and your only hope is that God will see his way to helping you out, then the only prayer for it was a "lament", a psalm of sorrow:

My God, my God, why have you forsaken me? Why are you so far from saving me, so far from the words of my groaning? (Psalm 22:1)

Maybe it's a sign of the troubles the Israelites had over the years that by far the largest group of psalms are the laments!

9 The Day of Atonement

"Festival" doesn't quite conjure up the right picture for the Day of Atonement, or *Yom Kippur* as it is known in Hebrew. It wasn't a fun day, and it wasn't meant to be. It was (and still is) the day on which the whole nation of Israel admitted to God that they'd let him down and prayed for his forgiveness.

On this day atonement will be made for you, to cleanse you. Then, before the Lord, you will be clean from all your sins. (Leviticus 16:30)

The day was so serious that it was the only day in the year that the priest was allowed into the "Holy of Holies", so as to offer special prayers. It was regarded as the day on which God passed judgement on what every individual had been up to and, as a result, decided who was going to live and who was going to die in the year to come. It took him some time too. Judging was supposed to begin ten days before (on the first day of the Jewish New Year) and end on the day of *Yom Kippur* itself.

10 The scapegoat

If you're made the scapegoat for something, it means you get the blame – even if you didn't do it! (If you've got brothers or sisters you probably know the feeling... or they do!)

The term comes from the Old Testament. It was part of the rites carried out by the priests on the Day of Atonement. Two goats were chosen. For one of them it was a Bad News Day. For the other it was a Worse News Day. The priest tossed up (or the Old Testament equivalent) and decided which goat would be which.

The bad news goat got sacrificed to God as a sin-offering. This was a sacrifice for those times when the Israelites had done wrong accidentally.

The worse news goat still died, but nothing like as quickly. This was called the scapegoat. It was the more important of the two because it represented the sins of the whole nation. But it wasn't chopped up. Instead, the scapegoat was sent out into the desert – where it died of starvation.

BIBLICAL AND MIND-BOGGLING: NO. 7

The sling-shot really was used in Old Testament times – and it wasn't a toy. It was a weapon actually used in battle. Soldiers in the Egyptian, Syrian, Assyrian, Persian armies used it. Even hired soldiers in the Roman army used it!

What happened next?
David – The Story Continues

There's more to the story of David and Goliath than the usual lesson that God would always look after the Israelites if they were faithful to him. David was special. God had already decided that Saul wasn't a good enough king and had chosen David as the one who was going to take over from him one day. The story of his fight against Goliath is part of the heroic picture built up for him.

This isn't to say that the Old Testament writers were blind to David's faults. Far from it! As you'll see in the first and second Books of Samuel, David's life had more ups and downs than most... After beating Goliath, David became a hero. Everybody loved him. Well, nearly everybody. The exception was King Saul, who got mighty jealous of all the hero-worship David was getting. When David discovered that he had hired a gang to murder him, he decided it was time to play for another team. With the help of Saul's son, Jonathan, David escaped and became an outlaw.

In fact, David became a very successful outlaw! In between surviving umpteen attempts by Saul to kill him off he still found time to become even more of a hero by protecting Israelites, from marauding armies.

Saul died, and after many twists and turns (sometimes of the necks of Saul's descendants) David became King of Judea then, finally, King of all Israel.

David won so many battles against the Philistines and others that the Israelites became stronger than they'd ever been in their history.

David took a fancy to Bathsheba, the wife of Uriah, one of his soldiers. This was definitely not allowed (see 10 Commandments, No. 7). Hearing a little while later that she was expecting a baby, David secretly sent orders that Uriah should be sent into battle. Worse than that, when the attack began, everybody was to nip off and leave Uriah to fight on his own. This happened and, of course, Uriah was killed. David promptly married Bathsheba.

God was more than a bit annoyed. David repented, said sorry to God, and he and Bathsheba had another son. His name was Solomon, and he was destined to become almost as famous as his dad.

Solomon becomes King of Israel after David, and generally makes a good job of it. He's full of wisdom and the country prospers. He gets stuck into some big projects. The most important was to finish one that his father David had planned – the building of a temple at Jerusalem. From that day to this, Jerusalem is known as "The Holy City".

All this building took a lot of money and effort, so Solomon taxed his own people and introduced slave labour. In spite of the fact that this is just what God had said would happen to them if they had a king, the Israelites started complaining.

They were still complaining when Solomon died and his son, Rehoboam, took over. And when Rehoboam carried on in the same way, that was it. Enough was enough. The northern tribes, deciding that their patience and everything else had been taxed far enough, decided to set up their own kingdom with their own king. From then on, the northern part of the country was known as Israel and the southern part known as Judah.

The fortunes of the various kings of Israel and Judah are told 1 Kings and 2 Kings. Apart from talking about what went on during their reigns, these two books also pass judgement on how successful the various kings were:

– a king who got his people to worship God was a GOOD king.

– a king who allowed or – worse – encouraged his people to worship other gods was a BAD king.

According to the Old Testament there were a few good kings, but an awful lot of bad ones, the worst of the lot being Ahab. He was the king of Israel who did the BADDEST things, the baddest of all being to marry a woman named Jezebel...

STORY 8: JEZEBEL
(1 KINGS 16:29 - 2 KINGS 9:37)

Jezebel was a Baal-worshipper. Baal was not just one god, but many. There were boy baals and girl baals, and, according to the religion, each controlled a different part of nature. Hadad was the name of the big-Baal, because he controlled the weather. Pleasing him was essential if you wanted a good harvest and plenty of cornflakes. Hadad's mother was Asherah, who was the goddess of mothers and of the sea. Presumably you worshipped her if you wanted a big, bouncing baby with wavy hair!

Jezebel's religion gave Ahab a problem. As a King of Israel, he was supposed to worship the God. But if he did what he was supposed to do and worshipped God, then he got nagged something rotten by Jezebel.

On the other hand, if Ahab didn't worship God then he got nagged by Elijah – and Elijah was red-hot at nagging as well. He was one of God's prophets, people who were specially called to nag on God's behalf. Needless to say, Jezebel and Elijah weren't the best of friends...

BEST OF ENEMIES

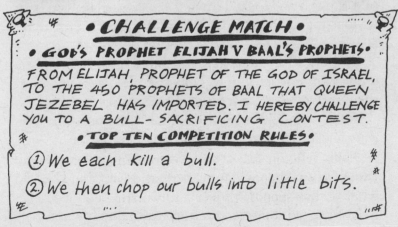

③ I go off to sit down.

④ Baal's prophets call on Baal to bring down fire (a fire-baal, ho·ho!) and burn up your bull as a sacrifice.

⑤ You've got all day to do it.

⑥ If you manage to call down fire, you win.

⑦ If you don't then it's my turn. I will soak my bull's bits in water — not once, not twice, but three times.

⑧ I will call on God to bring down fire.

⑨ If that happens, I win.

⑩ If I can't do it either, then we've got a problem. Not as big a problem as the two bulls though.

The challenge was accepted. The bulls were killed and cut up. Out came Baal's prophets. They sang and they danced all day but not a flicker.

Then it was Elijah's turn. He put his bull's bits on a pile of wood and soaked them three times. He even built a moat round the wood pile and filled that with water too. Then he called on God to send down fire.

God did as Elijah asked and more. Not only did he send down enough fire to burn the bull's bits and burn the wood, he even sent enough to burn up the water!

Elijah was proclaimed the winner and Baal's prophets were caught by the crowd and slaughtered.

Ahab was in the crowd and was very impressed. "Elijah turned in a scorching performance, dear," he told Jezebel when he got home.

Jezebel wasn't impressed. She wrote Elijah a note:

Dear Elijah.

I suppose you think you're very clever. Well I still think your religion is a load of bull.

Jezebel.

P.S. If you come back here I'll have <u>YOU</u> chopped to bits.

"Oh, gored!" exclaimed Elijah when he got the note. He decided to hide out in the land of Judah for a while and let the heat die down.

Jezebel promptly got up to a bit more of the nasty stuff. Ahab quite fancied owning a vineyard that was next to his palace. He wanted to use it for growing vegetables. So he wrote to the owner, a man named Naboth.

Dear Naboth,

Sell me your vineyard, there's a good chap. King Ahab.

Naboth replied at once.

Dear King Ahab,

I have considered your offer carefully but have decided that I want to care for it myself and not be careless and sell it to you.

In other words, you've had it mate — you can't have it!

Naboth.

165

When Jezebel saw Naboth's reply she wasn't pleased with her husband. So she told him "If you want your vegetable garden, you great turnip, you're going to have to play dirty!" So she got out her own writing pad and, pretending to be Ahab, rattled off a quick letter to the leaders of Naboth's town.

Dear Sirs,

I hear you're having a bit of bother in your town. Well it's all the fault of a guy called Naboth. What you should do is this:

1. Nab Naboth.
2. Put him on trial.
3. Get two liars to say that the bother's all Naboth's fault. (I'd be only too happy to recommend some reliable liars if it helps.)
4. Proclaim Naboth guilty as charged.
5. Have him stoned to death.

signed King Ahab himself, not Jezebel. I don't know anything about this letter.

P.S. Let me know when it's done

The scheme worked. Poor old Naboth got stoned and Ahab got his vineyard for nothing. This was too much for Elijah. Back he came, blazing mad and firing prophecies from all directions.

To cut a long story short, it all came true. An army general called Jehu (supported by Elijah's successor, Elisha) sets up a revolution. In quick succession, he pops off:

167

1 Ahab and Jezebel's son-in-law, the King of Judah.
2 Ahab and Jezebel's grandson.
3 Ahab and Jezebel's 42 other grandsons.
4 All 70 of Ahab's sons, having their heads delivered to him in baskets.
5 Anyone else in Ahab's family that he'd missed.

In the middle of this lot, Jehu sets off in search of Jezebel. She puts on her queenly make-up and comes to her window.

The conversation is brief:

"Yoo-hoo, Jehu! Are you going to kill me too?"

"Nope."

"Oh, good. Aaaaagggghhh!"

Jezebel's servants had saved Jehu the trouble by pushing her out of the window. Pausing only to run over her in his chariot, Jehu went indoors for his dinner. It must have been a good one, because before he'd finished he ordered the servants to scrape Jezebel up and give her a decent burial.

Too late. By the time they got out there, Elijah's final prophecy had been fulfilled. Wild dogs had already eaten everything except for Jezebel's skull, feet and hands. From then on, Baal worship was removed from Israel and Judah!

BIBLICAL BUT TRIVIAL: NO. 8

Jezebel and her make-up have gone down in history. An unlady-like lady who wears too much of the stuff is often called a "painted Jezebel".

FANTASTIC FACTS 8: WOMEN'S RIGHTS

Women rarely play leading roles in the Old Testament stories. They are mostly in the background. But this is not because they were regarded as inferior. The opening part of the *Book of Genesis* makes it clear that the two sexes were equal in the eyes of God.

So God created man in his own image, in the image of God he created him; male and female he created them. (Genesis 1:27)

In the same way, they were *both* to blame for what happened in the Garden of Eden. God didn't just boot out Eve and the serpent, he kicked out Adam as well!

So why do women tend to take a back seat? Almost certainly because it was a case of brawn before brains. The ancient world was a "man's world" where physical strength counted for more than anything else. When it came to ploughing fields in peacetime, or cutting heads off in wartime, men usually did a better job. This didn't just apply to the Hebrew world but to everywhere else as well.

Hebrew women were better off than most, in fact. Being thought of as the "weaker sex" meant that they were protected by law. That's part of what being under the authority of a man meant – that the man would care for the woman because it was his duty.

In spite of all this, plenty of women pop up in the Bible stories. When they do, they're just like the men: some are good, some are bad – and some are even worse! A few, like Eve, Rebecca and Delilah – we've met already. So here are another ten!

1 Sarah

Sarah was Abraham's wife. She was good-looking, too. In fact she was so good-looking that when Abraham took her with him to Egypt he asked her not to admit she was his wife in case somebody bumped him off out of jealousy!

God had made Abraham a promise: that he would be the father of the Hebrew nation. So, when Sarah reached the age of about 75 and still hadn't had a baby, she decided that God's promise probably wasn't going to come true! So she persuaded Abraham to take her servant Hagar as his wife as well. He did, and Hagar had a son named Ishmael.

15 years later, Sarah, now aged 90 discovered that she hadn't waited long enough!

God also said to Abraham … your wife Sarah will bear you a son, and you will call him Isaac. I will establish my covenant with him… (Genesis 17:15-19)

Sarah laughed when she heard, but the promise came true. No wonder the name Isaac means "the laughing one"!

Sarah lived to be 129 and is held up as an example of a woman who showed great faithfulness to her husband.

2 Hagar

What about Hagar, the servant and mother of Abraham's son, Ishmael? Well, Sarah may have been faithful but she wasn't prepared to share her husband. She told Abraham to send both Hagar and Ishmael off into the desert.

This wasn't the first time Hagar had been sent packing. After letting Abraham take her as his wife, Sarah had had second thoughts. "It's her or me!" she told Abraham. So Hagar had gone, only to be sent back by an angel who told her she was expecting Abraham's baby.

Then she'd been welcomed back, but now because Sarah did not want her son to share Abraham's inheritance with anybody, Hagar was sent off again. Soon Hagar's water ran out. She sat Ishmael under a bush and waited for them both to die. They didn't.

The angel of God called to Hagar from heaven. "Do not be afraid; God has heard the boy crying ... take him by the hand, for I will make him a great nation" (Genesis 21:17-18)

Hagar at once saw a well, collected as much water as they needed, and carried on. Ishmael grew up to be the father of a fellow tribe to the Hebrews, named the Ishmaelites.

3 Dinah

Girls sometimes think they're unlucky if they've got one brother. So what Dinah thought can only be imagined: she had twelve brothers!

Dinah was the daughter of Jacob, and the sister of his twelve sons. (Joseph was one of them, remember?) The story in the Old Testament about Dinah shows that while her brothers may have been a mean bunch to Joseph, they were even meaner to outsiders!

In the story, Dinah is attacked and dragged off against her will by a man named Shechem. He then says he wants to marry her. Enter the mean and crafty brothers!

"We can't give our sister to a man who's not circumcised. That would be a disgrace to us. We will give our consent to you on one condition only: that you become like us by circumcising all your males." (Genesis 34:14-15)

Well, Shechem and his dad must have been pretty good talkers because all the men of his town agreed. So, the operation was carried out. They were all circumcised – an operation in which the loose skin is cut from around their dangly bits – and promptly staggered off to bed to recover. Enter the brothers again!

Three days later, while all of them were still in pain... Simeon and Levi, Dinah's brothers, took their swords and attacked the unsuspecting city, killing every male. (Genesis 42:25)

Ouch!

4 Miriam

Miriam was the sister of Moses. Sadly, where he was a super-goody, Miriam is a not-so-goody. Her problem was that she was jealous of Moses. Now you might think that's understandable. Having a brother who's a leader, miracle worker, ace mountain climber, brilliant guide – and able to chat with God whenever he wants – must have made Miriam feel she couldn't win at anything. But that wasn't the point. Moses  was chosen by God, so for Miriam to be jealous of him was the same as her being jealous of God. Not on.

It wasn't always that way. Without Miriam, Moses wouldn't have survived. It was she who built his reed basket and sent him sailing down the River Nile to be picked up by the Pharaoh's daughter. Then, years later during the Exodus, it was Miriam who led the celebrations after the crossing of the Red Sea. She was called a prophetess.

That's when the jealousy set in. Together with her brother, Aaron, she began suggesting they were Moses' equals.

Miriam and Aaron began to talk... "Has the Lord spoken only through Moses?" they asked. "Hasn't he also spoken through us?" And the Lord heard this. (Numbers 12:1-2)

Miriam promptly caught leprosy – and had to depend on Moses asking God to make her better.

5 Deborah

Deborah was a multi-talented working wife! She was a judge who settled disputes:

She held court under the palm of Deborah… *and Israelites came to her to have their disputes decided.*
(Judges 4:5)

She was also the leader of the army – which meant she was no softy! When the Israelites were threatened by the Canaan army, Deborah called her general, Barak, and told him to go and fight them. What did the weed say?

"If you go with me, I will go; but if you don't go with me, I won't go." (Judges 4:8)

Going along for the battle, Deborah then proved to be a prophetess as well. She told Barak that God was supporting this battle, and that he couldn't lose. She even told him where to hold the battle. Barak found out who was the boss – everything she'd said came true.

Deborah was called a "mother in Israel", so perhaps after this she actually went home and cooked the tea. Her name means "bee", and it's certainly difficult to think of anyone in the Old Testament who was much busier.

6 Jael

This lady finishes off the previous story. Although Deborah's army won the battle, the Canaanite army commander, a fearsome soldier named Sisera, managed to escape. On the run, he met Jael who invited him to hide out in her tent. Thinking he was safe, he told Jael to watch out for his pursuers while he had a little sleep. Unfortunately for Sisera, he's the one who should have watched out.

Jael ... picked up a tent peg and a hammer and went quietly to him while he lay fast asleep, exhausted. She drove the peg through his temple into the ground. (Judges 4:21)

It also adds, a bit unnecessarily, that he died. Bad snooze!

7 Ruth

Get out the handkerchiefs. Ruth's story is one of the big romantic weepies in the Old Testament. Ruth wasn't an Israelite like her mother-in-law, Naomi, but a Moabite. When both women became widows, Naomi told Ruth that she was going back to Israel and that Ruth should leave her and carry on her own life. Ruth told Naomi in the nicest possible way that she had another thing coming:

Wherever you go, I will go, wherever you live, I will live. Your people shall be my people, and your God, my God. (Ruth 1:16)

But two women alone were going to have a hard time unless they found a man to protect them. While working in the fields Ruth met one of Naomi's relatives, named Boaz. Now the law says that a man's nearest relative has the right to buy that man's property – including his widow! – when he dies. Ruth quite fancied Boaz, so she suggested that he should get his money out and start buying.

The trouble was, Boaz was not their nearest relative! He told Ruth that someone else had the right to buy her. When Ruth recovered from the shock, Boaz went off to see the man who had this right and managed to talk him out of taking up his right. So Boaz married Ruth, Naomi moved in with the happy couple, and they all lived happily ever after. Ah!

8 Judith* 177

Judith lived a quiet life until the day her town was threatened with invasion by the massive Assyrian army. Furious with the leaders of the town (all men!) for sending word to the Assyrians that they'd surrender without a fight, Judith gave them a good tongue-lashing about their lack of faith in God. Then, after praying for God's help, she set out to do something about the Assyrians.

* The Book of Judith is one of the Apocryphal books.

Pretending to be a deserter, Judith managed to get close to their general-in-chief, a big-headed man named Holoferne. She told him what a star he was – and he believed it, of course. He then threw a party to celebrate the coming walkover against Judith's town. Holo might well have been hollow, he drank so much.

When he finally collapsed onto his bed, Judith joined him. But it wasn't for a kiss and a cuddle as he'd expected…

She went up to the bedpost by Holoferne's head and took down his scimitar; coming closer to the bed she caught him by the hair and said, "Make me strong today, Lord God of Israel!"… and cut off his head. (Judith 13:6-9)

Popping Holoferne's head into her food bag, Judith legged it straight home and showed it to the leaders of her town. Result – she was proclaimed a heroine and the Assyrians got whacked in the battle the next day.

9 Esther

Esther was a Jewish girl who'd been deported with her family to Babylon. She was obviously a good-looker because when the Babylonian king, Ahaseurus, decided he wanted the most beautiful girl in the land for his queen, Esther won the competition.

Then things got a bit tricky. Esther's father, Mordecai, had offended the King's top man, Haman. In revenge, crafty Haman persuaded the King to let him hang a group of people who were causing trouble.

"There is a certain people whose customs are different ... and who do not obey the king's laws." (Esther 3:8)

What he didn't mention was that he was talking about Esther's people, the Jews! So the King agreed.

Esther solved the problem, though. She invited Haman to dinner, without telling him she'd also invited the King – and while they were eating she spilt the beans! When the King found out that by agreeing to Haman's proposal he'd been tricked into condemning his own wife to death, he changed his mind sharpish.

As for Haman, he got it in the neck. He was hanged on the very scaffold he had prepared for Mordecai.

10 The widow with the pot of oil

There are a large number of unnamed women who make fleeting appearances in the Bible and then never appear again. One of them was the wife of a faithful man in the time of the prophet Elisha.

When the woman's husband died, leaving her and her two children with nothing to live on, she asked Elisha for help. On being asked what she had in her house, the woman told him that all she had was a little oil.

Elisha's command was curious. He told her to collect as many jars as she could, then go home and fill them with oil from her own little jar. She did, and the oil miraculously kept flowing until every jar was filled.

She went and told the man of God, and he said, "Go, sell the oil and pay your debts. You and your sons can live on what is left." (2 Kings 4:7)

That's it. The woman doesn't appear again. She doesn't even say, thanks!'

BIBLICAL AND MIND-BOGGLING: NO. 8

One of the Apocryphal books puts women firmly in their place. It's a poetic book called The Wisdom of Solomon which talks about how wondeful the gift of wisdom is. Here are a couple of lines from chapter 6, verse 12:

Wisdom is bright, and does not grow dim.
By those who love HER, SHE is readily seen.
Yes, wisdom is a female quality!

What happened next...?
After Jezebel and Ahab, things staggered on in pretty much the same way for a while. Rulers of Israel and Judah came and went, most of them according to the Old Testament being BAD.

Prophets came and went, too. Like Elijah and Elishah with Ahab and Jezebel, a prophet's role in life was to go out on behalf of God to tell the rulers and the people when they were being BAD, and what terrible things would happen to them if they didn't change their ways.

So did that mean the prophets were always GOOD?

Yes.

Except that sometimes they started off by being BAD...

181

STORY 9: JONAH
(BOOK OF JONAH)

Jonah was a reluctant prophet. He's asked by God to go and preach to the people of Nineveh, the capital of Israel's bitter enemies, Assyria. But Jonah doesn't fancy it. This is Story number nine…

A WHALE OF A TIME

"Jonah," said God one day, "I want you to go somewhere for me."

"Oh, yes?" said Jonah, suspiciously. "Where?"

"To Nineveh."

"Ohhhhh, no," said Jonah, "not Nineveh. N-O-T, NOT. Definitely not. Not Nineveh. Anywhere but Nineveh."

Jonah was not keen on going to Nineveh. "I mean, come on," said Jonah, "have you got any idea what the people are like in Nineveh? They're awful! Terrible!"

"Of course, I know what they're like in Nineveh!" said God. "Why do think I'm asking you to go there? I want you to warn them that unless they change their ways I'll destroy their city. So, come on! Move!"

Jonah moved all right. In the opposite direction. At the Port of Joppa there was a ship that was about to leave for Tarshish. Jonah bought his ticket, got on board, and settled down in the hold for a snooze.

"Great," he thought, "God won't find me down here."

Wrong, of course. That's one of the things about an all-seeing, all-round God. He knows what you're up to, wherever you are. And when he's able to whip up a storm at a moment's notice, then you're really in trouble.

Soon the wind was howling and the waves were crashing. The ship's crew started praying to their own gods. The captain woke Jonah up and told him to do the same. No use.

The sailors began to get a sinking feeling. "It must be a curse! Somebody on board must be responsible!" they cried. So they drew lots to discover who it was. Jonah won – or lost. He got picked, anyway.

"So it's you!" they all yelled. "This storm is all your fault! What have you done?"

"Nothing much," said Jonah. "I mean, I'm running away from God, who just happens to be the same God who made the heavens and the land and the sea…"

"The sea? You're trying to run away from the God of the sea?" The crew all turned on Jonah. "No wonder we're sinking!"

"Sorry, chaps," said Jonah. He could see now that it was all his fault. There was only one thing to do. He turned to the sailors, who'd been chucking things overboard to try to make the ship lighter. "Chuck me into the sea," he said. "You'll see. God will make it calm again then."

"We can't do that!"

"You must," said Jonah.

So, praying that Jonah's death wouldn't be held against them, they picked him up and tossed him over the side. Immediately God calmed the sea – and the sailors were so impressed that they adopted him as *their* God at once!

None of this helped Jonah, who thought he was going to drown. He'd forgotten that the God who made the sea had made the fish as well. Along came a big one and, at God's command, it swallowed Jonah whole.

So, what do you do when you've been swallowed by a giant fish and you think you've had your chips? Pray, that's what. Not for some salt and vinegar or a pickled onion, but for forgiveness.

"I'm a poor wretched sea-weed, God," said Jonah. "I deserved to drown. Thanks for saving me. Oh, yes. And I'll go to Nineveh for you."

"Fair enough," said God. "Let him go, fish!"

Well, there's only two ways out of a fish – the back way and the front way. Jonah may not have been too pleased to have been spewed up on the beach, but it had to be better than the alternative!

So, Jonah travelled to the wicked city of Nineveh and told the people there that if they didn't change their ways God would destroy them – and they had just forty days to stop him.

Jonah did a good job. Led by their king, the people of Nineveh *did* change their ways. For forty days they ate nothing, dressed in sackcloth as a sign of their sorrow, and prayed to God for forgiveness.

And, just as he had when Jonah had said sorry when he was inside the fish, God said, "Fair enough."

Jonah was *not* pleased. "You old softie!" he yelled. "I knew you'd forgive them! That's why I didn't want to come here in the first place."

So Jonah went off, to the outskirts of Nineveh, to sit down and began to sulk. It was hot and sunny. So God made a plant grow up to give Jonah some shade.

The next day, though, he told a worm to destroy it. The plant promptly died, leaving Jonah hot and miserable again.

"That's not fair," said Jonah. "I liked that plant!"

"You didn't make it," said God. "So why should you care about it. I, on the other hand, *did* make the people of Nineveh. So don't be angry if I care enough about them to forgive them!"

There's a lot to the story of Jonah. Most people only remember the bit about the fish, and think it's teaching a lesson about obeying God when he asks you to do something. In fact the important bit is at the end. When the people of Nineveh say they're sorry and change their ways, God forgives them. He refuses to destroy their city, saying at the same time that it wouldn't be fair on the innocent children or the animals.

BIBLICAL BUT TRIVIAL: NO. 9

The story is usually known as "Jonah and the Whale", but the Old Testament doesn't mention a whale, only a "big fish". But, if Jonah was swallowed by a whale then it would have had to be a sperm whale. This is because, although there are whales that are bigger than the sperm whale, none of them could actually swallow a man as their throats are like small fish-strainers. Those whales that are smaller than a sperm aren't big enough to hold a whole man in their stomach.

So a sperm whale it must have been.

No wonder Jonah blubbered so much!

FANTASTIC FACTS 9: PROPHET PROBLEMS

A prophet's job was to tell the Hebrews what God was thinking. The trouble was that not all of them were true prophets; a lot were "false prophets" who hadn't been selected by God.

So how did one become a prophet? Could anybody volunteer to be a prophet? Was the job advertised? Was there any training? Was a prophet's life very prophet-able? Here are your 10 Best considerations…

10 Best Tips: How to be a true prophet

1 Don't call God, he'll call you. A true prophet didn't decide to set up in business on his own. He had to be "called" by God.

2 Get a good night's sleep. Calls came in different ways, often through dreams or visions.

3 Turn down the offer. Like Jonah, most prophets told God they didn't want to be a prophet, thank you. They found out that God didn't take "No" for an answer

4 Be persuasive. A prophet didn't only listen to God; God

listened to him and made things happen

5 Practise hard. Prophets often gave "signs" to the people that they were true prophets, like calling down fire from the sky. This is why no. 4 was important; God produced the signs, so if he wasn't playing ball you were in trouble.

6 Keep up with the news. It was a prophet's job to look at what was happening ("the signs of the times") and, because God was behind all that went on, say *why* it was happening.

7 Have your eyes tested. Prophets could *accurately* predict the future. This is what set them apart from the "false prophets" – their predictions proved to be wrong.

8 Learn your lessons. Every prophet was a teacher (but not every teacher is a

prophet – ask yours). They only taught one lesson, though: Love God and obey the Commandments.

9 Get used to being unpopular. Prophets often had to tell people things they didn't want to hear – usually that they'd deserted God and should stop being wicked.

10 Change your wardrobe. Because people often didn't want to listen, the prophets wore hair shirts. These were a sign of mourning and told the people that the prophet was in mourning – for them!

The top prophets fulfilled every one of these considerations, as you'll see in this next section of facts and stories. Stand by for a quick prophecy. I predict that the next section is entitled: 10 Best Old Testament Best Prophets…

10 BEST OLD TESTAMENT PROPHETS

1 Samuel

Samuel was a prophet in the time of King Saul, but he was called by God when he was only a boy. It happened in the middle of the night – and almost got him a telling off!

Samuel and his dad, a priest named Eli, were resting. Suddenly, Samuel heard his name being called. Thinking it was his dad calling, he rushed in to ask what he wanted – only to be sent back again as Eli said he hadn't called. It wasn't until the third time it happened that Eli twigged what was going on. *Then Eli realised that the Lord was calling the boy. So Eli told Samuel, Go and lie down, and if he calls you, say, "Speak, Lord, for your servant is listening."* (*1 Samuel 3:8-9*)

Samuel went on to be such a valued adviser to Saul that the king even got a witch to summon up his spirit for a quick consultation after he'd died! (After Samuel had died, not Saul! Then he wished he hadn't. Samuel prophesied that Saul would be with him the next day – and he was! See *1 Samuel 28: 3-25*)

2 Elijah

Elijah was the prophet who gave Jezebel and the priests of Baal such a hot time by calling on God to send down fire

during the bull contest. This sign, in front of a huge crowd, was just one of many he produced during his career to convince people that he was a true prophet.

Other signs had a much smaller audience. For example having incurred Jezebel's anger after predicting a famine, Elijah went off to hide. After being fed by ravens for a while, he then went off to a place called Zarephath. There he met a widow who didn't doubt that he was a prophet of God. As a reward, Elijah miraculously increased the small amount of bread and oil she had so that there was enough to feed them and the widow's son until the famine ended.

Elijah also spoke to God, many times. When the widow's son died, he asked:

"O Lord my God, let this boy's life return to him!" The Lord heard Elijah's cry, and the boy's life returned to him, and he lived. (1 Kings 17:2)

Elijah is one of the greatest of the prophets, as can be seen from the way the Old Testament says he died. Not for him the business of being buried...

Suddenly a chariot of fire and horses of fire appeared ... and Elijah went up to heaven in a whirlwind (2 Kings 2:11)

Being taken straight into heaven was the greatest honour that God could have given him – which must have left Elijah in a bit of a spin!

3 Elisha

Elisha was Elijah's successor, and he carried on with the prophecies of doom against Jezebel and Ahab and lived to advise many other kings of the time. He was different from other prophets in that he wasn't called by God directly; instead, God told Elijah to do the job:

So Elijah ... found Elisha ... went up to him and threw his cloak around him. (1 Kings 19:19)

Elisha didn't care that he'd been given a cloak of smelly old goat's hair. He knew that it was a sign that he'd been called as Elijah's successor. (In many Bible translations, the word cloak is given as "mantle". Hence the saying, still used today, of "taking up the mantle" – meaning taking on a job from somebody else.)

4 Micaiah

Micaiah was a chap who had to face stiff competition from a group of false prophets – 400 of them! King Ahab, the king of Israel, and his opposite number the King of Judah, Jehosophat, wanted to know if they should go and fight a battle against the King of Aram. The 400 told Ahab that he'd win a battle, no problem.

Jehosophat wasn't so sure, and called on Micaiah who said that not only would the battle be lost, but that King Ahab would get killed as well. This was not what Ahab wanted to hear!

Didn't I tell you he never prophesies anything good about me, only bad?... Put this fellow in prison and give him nothing but bread and water until I return safely. (1 Kings 22:18,27)

Ahab promptly got killed by a stray arrow and Micaiah, presumably, stayed in prison for ever! The Old Testament doesn't say he was let out, anyway.

5 Isaiah number 1

There are thought to have been two prophets named Isaiah, separated in time by some 200 years. Only the life of the first, Isaiah number 1, is detailed in the *Book of Isaiah*. He tells that his call came in a vision in which he actually saw God in the temple. Was he pleased? Not a bit of it. Nobody was perfect, so seeing the holy God face to face meant you were dead!

"Woe to me!" I cried. "I am ruined! For I am a man of unclean lips ... and my eyes have seen the King, the Lord Almighty!" (Isaiah 6:5)

Whether he was admitting to being somebody who'd told lies, dirty jokes, or what didn't matter. God solved the problem by sending one of his angels down to touch Isaiah's lips – with a red-hot coal! (Bet he was glad it was a vision.)

194

Isaiah preached God's message of "love your neighbour" to the leaders of Jerusalem, who had become very corrupt – and he didn't mince his words:

Woe to those who call evil good and good evil ... woe to those who are heroes at drinking wine and champions at mixing drinks, who acquit the guilty for a bribe, but deny justice to the innocent. (Isaiah 5:20-23)

He prophesied doom – that Israel and Judah would be conquered by the Assyrians – but he also prophesied hope so long as the people followed God.

The people walking in darkness have seen a great light; on those living in the land of the shadow of death a light has dawned. (Isaiah 9:2)

In the tradition of the prophets, Isaiah performed signs as well. He gave one to a king named Hezekiah – who'd prayed to be cured from an illness – to show that his prayers had been answered: he made the sun go backwards!

6 Isaiah number 2

ISAIAH ONE OR ISAIAH TWO? DID I EXIST? IT'S OVER TO YOU!

Here's a prophet with a difference – there's no certainty that he ever lived!

The *Book of Isaiah* is very long, it has 66 chapters. The first 39 chapters talk about Israel and Judah before they were attacked by Assyria. But then there's a jump, and chapters 40 onwards talk about the time when the Israelites were exiled to Babylon, some 200 years later.

So, either Isaiah was absolutely brilliant at predicting *or* somebody else – a mysterious Isaiah number 2 living at the time of the exile – wrote them and tacked them on to the end of the book. There's no real agreement.

What is clear, though, is that the later part shows a prophet who isn't telling his people to buck their ideas up. In Babylon, the Israelites had hit rock-bottom. Isaiah 2 is doing the other side of a prophet's job; he's telling them that one day they'll be allowed to go back home again.

But now, this is what the Lord says – he who created you, O Jacob, he who formed you, O Israel: Fear not, for I have redeemed you; I have summoned you by name; you are mine. (Isaiah 43:1)

7 Jeremiah

Out of all the prophets, Jeremiah was the one who had to get used to not being liked. God made him prophesy doom and gloom for 40 years!

He was explaining "the signs of the times" and what he saw was that Judah would fall and that Jerusalem would be destroyed. Now, imagine somebody wandering round your town for 40 years saying that it was going to be smashed up by invaders. Don't you think somebody would try to shut him up?

They certainly tried to shut Jeremiah up. In his time he was put in the stocks, thrown into prison and lowered to the bottom of a muddy well and left to die. No wonder he wished he'd never been born!

Alas my mother, that you gave me birth, a man with whom the whole world strives and contends! I have neither lent nor borrowed, yet everyone curses me. (Jeremiah 15:10)

In the end, though, he was able to say "Told you so!" Proving that he was a true prophet, Jerusalem was destroyed.

8 Ezekiel

The prophet Ezekiel was a man of vision: he couldn't stop having them!

He was exiled to Babylon, and that's where his call to be prophet came. He had an amazing vision of four winged creatures flying towards him carrying God's throne ... and God was sitting in it! At least, that was what Ezekiel thought:

I saw that from what appeared to be his waist up he looked like glowing metal, and from there down he looked like fire; and a brilliant light surrounded him. Like the appearance of a rainbow in the clouds on a rainy day, so was the radiance around him. (Ezekiel 1:27-28)

So it's not surprising that his key message is also described with some amazing imagery. Ezekiel finds himself in a valley littered with dry bones which God tells him represent the dead Israel. He then tells him:

This is what the sovereign Lord says to these bones: I will make breath enter you and you will come to life... I

will make flesh come upon you and cover you with skin...
(Ezekiel 37:4-6)

It all sounds a bit like emergency surgery, but the message Ezekiel preached was that it meant God would be bringing them to life again and making sure they returned from exile one day.

9 Hosea

When God spoke, a true prophet did what he was told – even if it meant bringing trouble on himself. And Hosea got plenty of trouble!

God told the prophet Hosea that he should get married. Fine so far – until God added that he had to marry a woman who would make a fool of him by running away from him and going to another man. Hosea agreed! What's more, he didn't have any trouble finding such a wife, so wicked were the people where he lived. Sure enough, his wife ran off. So why the command? So that Hosea could experience some misery, and then write about how God felt about the same sort of misery when his "wife" Israel went off to worship other gods. Hosea is then told to take his wife back again – for the same reason; so that he can write about God's forgiveness.

My heart is changed within me; all my compassion is aroused. I will not carry out my fierce anger. (Hosea 11:8-9)

Talk about a marriage made in heaven!

10 Haggai

Some prophets served for a long time, others for a lot less. Haggai was a prophet for three months – which might explain why the Book of Haggai is the shortest in the Old Testament.

At the time of writing, the people had returned to Jerusalem from exile. Initially full of enthusiasm, they started to rebuild the Temple, but then they slacked off. It was Haggai's job to tell them to get moving again.

"Is it a time for you yourselves to be living in your pannelled houses, while this house (the Temple) remains a ruin?... The glory of this present house will be greater than the glory of the former house," says the Lord Almighty. "And in this house I will grant peace."

The people listened and the Temple was finished. Haggai would have no trouble finding a job as a builder nowadays!

BIBLICAL AND MIND-BOGGLING: NO. 9

As a sign that Elijah is expected to come again one day, the table for the passover meal has a place set for him.

What happened next...?

As we've just seen, the constant theme of the prophets over the years was that the Hebrews, north and south, were going to get it in the neck for forgetting the covenant and deserting God. In the end, the prophets were all proved right. (That's how we know they were prophets!)

After the split into Israel and Judah, the two separate nations continued to be the target for take-over bids. Israel was the first to go, swallowed by Assyria in 721 BC, just as the prophet Amos had predicted:

Israel has fallen, never to rise again! She lies abandoned on the ground, and no one helps her up! (Amos 5:2)

Judah lasted longer. Much of their land was taken over by the Assyrians. In the eyes of the prophet Isaiah, this was God's punishment:

God says: I use Assyria like a club to punish those with whom I am angry. I sent Assyria to attack a godless nation. (Isaiah 10:5).

Obviously the people bucked their ideas up a bit, because when the Assyrians laid siege to Jerusalem in 701 BC they successfully resisted.

They bucked their ideas up even more in 621 BC, when an amazing discovery was made during repairs to the Temple in Jerusalem. A battered old book was found. It was what is now called the *Book of Deuteronomy*, which lists all the laws that the people should have been obeying if they'd been keeping their side of the Covenant with God. It's pretty clear they weren't doing too well. When he saw it, the king, Josiah promptly set about reforming things and getting the Judeans worshipping God again.

Did it help? Well, they didn't have any more trouble with Assyria... because the Assyrians' own days were numbered. A new force, the Babylonians were about to sort *them* out.

Prophets like Jeremiah had seen it all coming, of course. *God Almighty says: I am going to send for all the peoples from the north and for my servant, King Nebuchadnezzar of Babylonia. I am going to bring them to fight against Judah... This whole land will be left in ruins. (Jeremiah 25:9-11).*

In 596 BC, Jerusalem fell and Judah surrendered to Babylonia. To make sure they didn't have any more trouble from Judah's king or its leaders, the lot of them were exiled to Babylon.

But, ten years later, trouble was precisely what King Nebuchadnezzar *did* get. There was a revolt in Jerusalem and in went his army. This time they made sure there would be no more trouble. The city, including the Temple, was destroyed completely and the whole population exiled.

Stuck in Babylon, the exiled Hebrews finally realised that the prophets had been right all along. All their problems had been caused through deserting God and forgetting the Covenant. There and then they decided to change their ways and start worshipping their God again.

The trouble was, worshipping God wasn't allowed in Babylon...

STORY 10: DANIEL
(BOOK OF DANIEL)

As a young man, the prophet Daniel was carted off to Babylon and put into the service of successive Babylonian kings. The *Book of Daniel* tells the story of his battle to worship God and no other. This is the most famous part of Daniel's story. It concerns King Darius…

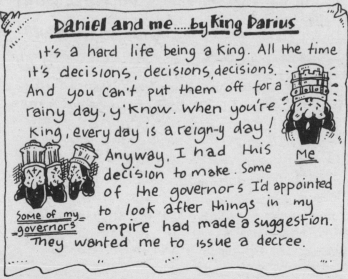

Daniel and me…..by King Darius

It's a hard life being a King. All the time it's decisions, decisions, decisions. And you can't put them off for a rainy day, y'know. When you're King, every day is a reign-y day!

Me

Anyway, I had this decision to make. Some of the governors I'd appointed to look after things in my empire had made a suggestion. They wanted me to issue a decree.

Some of my governors

Royal Decree

Let it be known that for the next 30 days no requests can be made of any god, or any man for that matter, except me.

signed.... King Darius.

Well, it looked fine to me. It meant extra work, of course, but I could see the logic behind it. If the people thought their problems could be solved by talking to any old god, Dick or Harry where would I be? Out of a job, that's where!

Even so, the punishment for disobeying the decree looked a bit on the harsh side.

PUNISHMENT FOR DISOBEYING THE ROYAL DECREE

Anybody disobeying the Royal Decree will be thrown into a pit filled with lions.

Signed by King Darius as well.

Phew! Talk about a penalty claws!

Anyway, I took my pen out – then stopped and had another think. It didn't do to be too hasty about these things. Once a Royal Decree was signed, that was it. There was no going back. The thing couldn't be unsigned. I mean, you'd be admitting you'd got it wrong and that would never do. Kings can't make mistakes. Well, we can, but nobody must know about it.

Eventually, though, I signed. Little did I know what I'd done. The whole thing had been a put-up job. My governors had dreamed up the whole scheme as a way of getting shot of Daniel.

Daniel was my favorite governor. Even though he was a Hebrew exile, he'd done very well. I'd been thinking seriously of making him boss. That's why the others were jealous of him.

DANIEL

They also knew he was as honest as they come, so they couldn't get him that way.

No his only weakness was that he insisted on praying to the god of the Hebrews three times a day. The other governors knew it. That's why they talked me into signing that Decree.

Next thing I knew, the governors were banging on my door. They'd caught Daniel in the act.

What could I do? Nothing.

205

DEATH WARRANT

I HEREBY ORDER THAT DANIEL BE CAST INTO THE LION'S PIT

Signed, and getting writer's cramp

King Darius

P.S sorry Daniel, I fought tooth and nail, but there was nothing I could do. May your God rescue you.

I went with Daniel as he was taken to the pit. I watched as they rolled a stone over the entrance. Then I put my royal seal on it so that nobody could come and rescue him. After that I went home to bed.

Bed? Hah! I couldn't sleep. All night long I kept imagining what was going on in that pit — and what was coming off! It was horrible. I'd tried counting sheep but every time I closed my eyes I found myself counting lions. The thought of what was happening to Daniel was tearing me apart.

As soon as it was light I got out of bed and hurried to the pit entrance

"Roll the stone away!" I commanded.

I braced myself for the worst. Slowly, I peered over the side and down into the pit.

"Morning." said Daniel.

"Daniel!" I cried "You're all right! And all left! You're all in one piece, in fact!"

Quickly we hauled him out of the pit. "Why didn't the lions attack you?" I asked. "They're not exactly pussy cats."

"God protected me," said Daniel. "He likes nothing better than a nice juicy problem to get his teeth into. He sent an angel to seal the lion's jaws."

I was relieved, I can tell you. The lions weren't so pleased though. They hadn't had their breakfast. So I fed those sneaky no-good governors to them instead.

Being king can be fun now and then.

The story of Daniel was important to the people of his time. Imagine yourself, stuck in the middle of a foreign land when all you want to do is to go back home again (especially as your teachers would have been exiled with you).

What you want is some hope that everything will be all right again. That's the message of this story. It tells the people to stand up to the bullying they were getting from their captors and have faith in God.

BIBLICAL BUT TRIVIAL: NO. 10

Daniel could be said to be the first lion tamer. The first lion-taming act in modern times took place in 1835 as part of a travelling circus known as "Wombwell's Menagerie". A man calling himself "Manchester Jack" sat on the back of an aged lion called Nero and stuck his hand in its mouth.

FANTASTIC FACTS 10: UNDER THE INFLUENCE

Even if you've never read a word of the Bible, the chances are you still know something about it – even before picking up this book.

Over the years the Bible has had an amazingly wide influence on all sorts of areas. Here's a 10 Best quiz. Maybe at the end of it you'll have discovered that you actually knew a lot more than you knew you knew…

1 Figures of speech
Many of our sayings or figures of speech are actually derived from the Bible. Here's a list of well-known sayings. Which 10 came from, or refer to, the Old Testament?

1 There's a fly in the ointment

2 He thinks he's the great I am

3 There's nothing new under the sun

4 Pride goes before a fall

5 Life lasts for three score years and ten

6 Many hands make light work

7 You can't take it with you when you go!

8 They've had it! The writing's on the wall!

9 I'm at my wits' end

10 Can a leopard change its spots?

11 They escaped by the skin of their teeth

12 Too many cooks spoil the broth

Answer:
Numbers 6 and 12 *don't* come from the Old Testament, the rest do. Here's where you'll find them:
1 – Ecclesiastes 10:1; 2 – Exodus 3:14 (where Moses asks God what his name is and is told "I am who I am"; 3 – Ecclesiastes 1:9; 4 – Proverbs 16:18; 5 – Psalm 90:10; 7 – Ecclesiastes 5:15; 8 – Daniel chap 5; 9 – Psalm 107:27; 10 – Jeremiah 13:23; 11 – Job 19:20

2 Books and poetry

Many famous works have been influenced by Old Testament stories. The story of Adam and Eve is the basis of the epic poem *Paradise Lost* by John Milton.

The classic story *Moby Dick* by Herman Melville, about a sea captain's hunt for a white whale, is full of

Biblical references. The basic plot (like that of the Old Testament) is about the struggle between good and evil. And, with the captain's name being *Ahab*, his ship called *Rachel*, two mad sailor prophets called *Elijah* and *Gabriel*, and the whole story being told by a wandering sailor called *Ishmael*, you can see where the author got his characters' names from!

3 Plays and films

If you haven't yet seen or read any Shakespeare plays don't worry – you will! And when you do, you're likely to meet the Old Testament as well. Shakespeare often used lines which referred to Old Testament stories. In his play *Henry IV, part 2* Shakespeare's character Sir John Falstaff tells the Lord Chief Justice:

I am as poor as Job, my Lord, but not so patient.
(Act 1, Scene 2)

Modern-day entertainment is still using the events of 3,000 years ago for ideas. Stacks of films have been based on Old Testament stories. They include *Samson and Delilah* (1949) and *The Bible... In The Beginning* (1966) – a long film which only covered the first 22 chapters of the *Book of Genesis*. The most famous of them all is probably *The Ten Commandments*, first made in 1923 and then again in 1956. (As most of these films were made in Hollywood, God always spoke with an American accent!)

Other films have taken Biblical ideas and built them into adventures. The question of what happened to the Ark of the Covenant when the Temple in Jerusalem was finally destroyed by the Romans in AD 70 is the theme of the rip-roaring Indiana Jones film, *Raiders of the Lost Ark*.

4 The law!

Modern-day laws owe a lot to the Ten Commandments. Stealing (no. 8) and murder (no. 6) are obviously crimes. Adultery (no. 7) is not a crime, but a married couple can get divorced if one partner commits adultery – just as was the case in Old Testament times. And bearing false witness (no. 9) is certainly a crime in a court of law; it's called perjury.

So is taking God's name in vain (no. 3) you may be surprised to learn. The crime of blasphemy is just that, and a person who stands in the middle of a shopping arcade and shouts rude things about God or the Bible can still be arrested!

Even the commandment to "Keep the Sabbath holy" (no. 4) still has some influence over the law. The Christian "Sabbath" is Sunday, which used to be a day when most shops weren't allowed to open. Now they all can, but only for six hours and not before 10 a.m.

5 Art

Some of the most famous paintings in the world depict Old Testament scenes. The Dutch artist, Rembrandt produced many dramatic masterpieces and drawings such as *Potiphar's Wife Accusing Joseph, Jacob Blessing the Sons of Joseph, The Finding of Moses, Moses Smashing the Commandments* and *The Blinding of Samson.*

Some Old Testament paintings weren't actually done on a canvas, but on a ceiling! The ceiling of the Sistine Chapel of St Peter's Basilica in Rome shows nine scenes from the *Book of Genesis,* including the *Creation of Adam,* the *Creation of Eve,* and the *Flood.* To do them, the artist Michaelangelo had to lie on his back on a scaffold for four years! (Hence the joke: Why was Michelangelo a contortionist? Because he could paint on his back!)

6 Names

This has been one of the longest-lasting influences. Perhaps you've got a biblical name?

Some of the many Old Testament names for boys that are still in common use today are: David (or Dave), Adam, Joseph (or Joe, Joey), Daniel (or Danny), Joshua (or Josh), Aaron, Benjamin (or Ben), Nathan, Jonathan (or John, Johnny) and Samuel (or Sam, Sammy).

Old Testament names for girls still around are: Sarah, Rebecca (or Becky), Deborah (or Debbie), Danielle (female version of Daniel), Rachel, Judith, Hannah, Miriam, Eve, Ruth and Josephine (or Jo – female version of Joseph).

They're not just chosen by a few parents for their children either. In 1993, the most popular names in Britain were Daniel for boys and Rebecca for girls.

7 Science
Until the 19th century, the Bible was taken to be a scientific book as well as a religious history. The account of the creation was assumed to be scientific fact – that the world and everything in it had been created by God in six days. When a man named Charles Darwin popped up with his *Theory of Evolution* – putting forward evidence that creatures had in fact developed slowly, changing to adapt themselves to life on earth, he caused a sensation!

Suddenly people had to look at the Old Testament again. When they did, they saw that the stories hadn't become any less true. Darwin's evidence didn't show that the world *hadn't* been created by God; what he'd done was to show that the Bible wasn't a scientific text book.

Since then the "evolution vs creation" argument has largely been assumed to have been won by the evolutionists. And yet, at different points in the chain of development there are points at which a species has taken an unexplained, and giant, leap forward.

8 Slavery

Not all Biblical influence has been for good. The slave trade which flourished in England and the United States until 1860 was perhaps the worst example. It showed that the Bible can sometimes be quoted by the supporters of both sides of an argument in an attempt to prove their case.

One church minister, a man named Thornton Stringfellow, actually wrote a sermon entitled "A Scriptural View of Slavery". One of his arguments was that slavery was allowed because it was included in the Ten Commandments! He did this by quoting the full text of the 10th Commandment:

You shall not covet your neighbour's house. You shall not covet your neighbour's wife, or his manservant *or* maidservant, *his ox or donkey, or anything that belongs to your neighbour. (Exodus 21:17)*

Against this, the anti-slavery campaigners quoted different parts of the Bible. They argued that the prophets had called for justice, saying that what God wanted was for the leaders of the country:

To lose the chains of injustice ... to set the oppressed free and break every yoke. (Isaiah 58:6)

The anti-slavery campaigners won!

9 Music

Music was greatly influenced by the Old Testament at that time. The slaves, mostly Africans who had been stolen by slave traders and shipped to America, saw their troubled life as being exactly the same as that of the Israelites in Egypt. Their hope that they, too, would be free one day showed in the development of "spirituals" or songs based on Bible stories.

Perhaps at the other extreme, many of the great composers were inspired to write operas based on Old Testament stories – such as Rossini's *Moses in Egypt* and Saint-Saen's *Samson and Delilah*. Leonard Bernstein (later to write the music for *West Side Story*, and the film version of Shakespeare's *Romeo and Juliet*) even set some of the prophet Jeremiah's moans and groans to music in his *Jeremiah Symphony*.

Pop music hasn't ignored the Old Testament either. The Israelites' exile in Babylonia was the theme of pop song *By the Rivers of Babylon* by the 1980s group "Boney M". It wasn't a dud either – it went to No. 1 in the charts!

10 Oops!

With so many different translations and copies of the Bible being produced, there have been a few biblical bloopers committed along the way. Such as:

● A 1612 version of the King James Bible which should have had Psalm 119:161 reading, *Princes have persecuted me without cause*, but instead had the brilliant misprint, *Printers have persecuted me without cause!*

● A 1631 Bible which left out the magic word "not" and left Commandment No. 7 saying, *Thou shalt commit adultery*.

● A 1966 Bible which should have had Psalm 122:6 saying, *Pray for peace in Jerusalem* but instead read *Pay for peace in Jerusalem!*

BIBLICAL AND MIND-BOGGLING: NO. 10

Nowadays you might associate lions with Africa and India, but not the Middle East. But in Old Testament times there were certainly lions in the Jordan valley. Assyrian kings did keep lions in pits and would regularly go out for a happy day's lion-hunting.

What happened next...?

Eventually, like all empire-builders, the Babylonians got beaten up themselves.

In 539 BC, led by a king named Cyrus, the Persians captured Babylon and took over the Babylonian empire.

The Persians allowed the Hebrews to go back to their homeland if they wanted. A small number of them did so, promising that they'd learned their lesson and that they'd worship God properly in future.

The idea of the Covenant was stronger than ever, now. After their years in exile the Hebrews had had time to think about something else that Jeremiah had said God would do:

The new covenant that I will make with the people of Israel will be this: I will put my law within them and write it on their hearts. I will be their God, and they will be my people. (Jeremiah 31:33)

So the people rebuilt the Temple in Jerusalem and tried again.

Here endeth the Old Testament
And that's where the Old Testament stories just about end. But…

Ever since the first time they were exiled, a teaching had been developing. Prophet after prophet had said that a special man – the Messiah would come and save the Israelites from their conquerors. One of them was the prophet Micah. He'd written: *Bethlehem, you are one of the smallest towns in Judah, but out of you I will bring a ruler for Israel. (Micah 5:1-12)*

An absolute star, born in Bethlehem? Yes, we're back in Bible Times again. But now it's the time of Jesus and the New Testament.

And that's another 10 Best stories!

THE END

IF YOU LIKE THIS, YOU MIGHT LIKE...

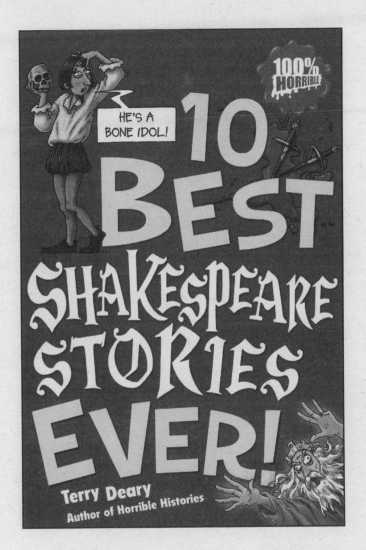